On the Altar

On the Altar

The call to be a living sacrifice

by

Jonathan Roberts

with reflections by
Jayne Roberts

The Salvation Army
UNITED KINGDOM TERRITORY
WITH THE REPUBLIC OF IRELAND
101 Newington Causeway, London SE1 6BN

On the Altar
Jonathan Roberts
First published in 2018 by
Shield Books
© The Salvation Army
United Kingdom Territory with the Republic of Ireland
101 Newington Causeway, London SE1 6BN

ISBN 978-1-911149-30-9
eISBN 978-1-911149-31-6

Project Editor: Major David Dalziel
Cover Design: Mark Knight

All rights reserved. No part of this publication may be reproduced, stored in a retrieval system, or transmitted in any form, or by any means, electronic, mechanical, photocopying, recording or otherwise without the prior written permission of the publisher.

Registered charity no. 214779, and in Scotland SC009359

Scripture quotations, unless otherwise stated, are from Holy Bible, New International Version® Anglicised, NIV® copyright © 1979, 1984, 2011 by Biblica, Inc.® Used by permission. All rights reserved worldwide.

SHIELD BOOKS
© The Salvation Army
United Kingdom Territory with
the Republic of Ireland

Printed by THQ Print and Design Unit

CONTENTS

Foreword		vii
Introduction		ix

PART ONE – A Picture of Sacrifice

Chapter 1	The Power of Pictures	3
Chapter 2	Orders and Regulations for Sacrifices	6
Chapter 3	Prophet and Loss	11
Chapter 4	A Living Metaphor	15
Chapter 5	The Sacrifice of Jesus	18
	Reflection One: The Sacrifice of Jesus	23

PART TWO – A Living Sacrifice

Chapter 6	Total Dedication	26
Chapter 7	True and Proper Worship	30
Chapter 8	Metamorphosis	33
Chapter 9	The Word and the Spirit	36
	Reflection Two: Dedication	39

PART THREE – Praying

Chapter 10	The Offering of Prayer	42
Chapter 11	Confessing	47
Chapter 12	Asking	51
Chapter 13	Listening	56
	Reflection Three: Praying	61

PART FOUR – Praising

Chapter 14	Let there be Praise!	64
Chapter 15	Praise and Worship: Is there a Difference?	67
Chapter 16	Let All Things their Creator Bless!	71
Chapter 17	A Costly Sacrifice	75
	Reflection Four: Praising	79

Part Five – Serving

Chapter 18	In the Ministry	82
Chapter 19	The Roots of Service	86
Chapter 20	Full Equipment for the Task	89
	Reflection Five: Serving	95

Part Six – Doing Good

Chapter 21	Do-gooders	98
Chapter 22	Love in Action	102
Chapter 23	Social Justice	107
Chapter 24	Sacrificial Good	111
	Reflection Six: Doing Good	115

Part Seven – Giving

Chapter 25	A Spiritual Issue	118
Chapter 26	Generous and Costly	121
Chapter 27	Counting the Cost	125
Chapter 28	Cheerful Giving	129
	Reflection Seven: Giving	133

Part Eight – Witnessing

Chapter 29	Use Words – They are Necessary!	136
Chapter 30	Come and See – Go and Tell!	139
Chapter 31	Proclaimers of the Gospel	143
Chapter 32	Opportunity Knocks!	146
Chapter 33	And You Will Receive Power	149
Chapter 34	A Priestly Duty	153
	Reflection Eight: Witnessing	157

In Conclusion	159
Endnotes	161

Foreword

A FEW years ago, after I had moved into a different culture, a young Christian gave me some unrequested advice: 'Don't preach about sacrifice here. It doesn't go down well.' I gently reminded him of Jesus' call to 'take up your cross and follow' and that to 'lose' our life for his sake was the best way to find it. It made no difference to him. Sacrificial living was not a good selling point – forget it!

In *On the Altar,* Jonathan Roberts doesn't set out to make it sound attractive, but he does skilfully put it into broad and compelling context. He also shows that the sacrificial dimension is an essential and ultimately enriching part of life.

His introduction gives immediate clues as to how the book might unfold, by drawing attention to a contrasting variety of motives that might inspire anyone to make various kinds of sacrifice – some more worthy than others. And so begins a journey during which the reader is invited to examine the way sacrifice was understood in the Old Testament, before moving on to consider the sacrificial life and death of Jesus, and then the implications of these for us today.

Using telling illustrations and challenging material from many sources, the writer guides us into intelligent consideration of the background information he provides, as well as urging us to respond to the implications of what it means to live for and with Christ. The Reflection pages at the end of each section, supplied by Jayne Roberts, further enhance this.

Very readable, with an uncomplicated style, the book covers its engaging variety of topics in inspiring and imaginative ways.

It is focused on the real world. Of the sacrifice of Jesus it states, 'It involved real giving, real obedience, real cost and achieved a real reconciliation with God.' We are invited to embrace the reality of what this may mean for us. I also encourage you to do so.

Robert Street
Commissioner

Introduction

SACRIFICE is not always a popular concept. In many parts of the world the emphasis is more often on self-fulfilment, self-gratification and self-improvement – all achieved by the easiest route possible. But the attitudes and actions of some people stand out from this. There are those who make sacrifices in order to reach a goal, such as top athletes who give their time, spend their energy and adopt a rigorous lifestyle to achieve success. We rightly admire them for their dedication and discipline.

Even so, we realise they are doing it for themselves. Their aim is to win a race, gain a medal and be recognised as 'the best'. Although sacrifice is involved, ultimately it can simply be another form of self-fulfilment.

At the other extreme are people who sacrifice their lives for others. Nations remember and honour those who 'gave their lives' for their country in times of war. And some give their lives – and lose their lives – for other people in times of peace.

In central London, near the place of John Wesley's conversion, is Postman's Park. A small and insignificant place, it is easily missed unless you are looking for it but it contains a moving tribute to 'heroic self-sacrifice'.

On one of the walls there are numerous plaques describing briefly how 'everyday heroes' lost their lives trying to save others. Here are just three:

> William Fisher, aged 9, lost his life on Rodney Road, Walworth, while trying to save his little brother from being run over, July 12, 1886.

> Mary Rogers, stewardess of the *Stella*, March 30, 1899, self-sacrificed by giving up her life belt and voluntarily going down in the sinking ship.

> Leigh Pitt, reprographic operator, aged 30, saved a drowning boy from the canal at Thamesmead, but sadly was unable to save himself, June 7, 2007.

Between the kind of sacrifice that eventually brings benefit to the people themselves and the kind that costs people their lives we find a wide range of self-giving acts that can be thought of as sacrificial. They carry with them the idea of cost, or even suffering, which will bring some good to the lives of others or some benefit to a cause people believe in.

Parents might deny themselves expensive holidays or a larger house in order to afford a better education for their children. People may be willing to do low-paid work or voluntary service in another country rather than taking a well-paid job at home. While there could be elements of self-interest even in such altruistic actions, the primary focus is on others.

Sacrifice is generally thought to be an admirable thing. As Colin Gunton says: 'A feeling of the rightness or even necessity of a sacrificial dimension to our existence runs very deep in human experience.'[1]

It seems that a society focused on self-fulfilment still sees value in self-sacrifice, even if most people would not want to embrace it for themselves! Could it be that people see in sacrifice something noble – even something holy?

This brings us to sacrifice as a spiritual concept and to the theme of this book, which is to explore what sacrifice means in the life of the Christian. The idea and practice of sacrifice go back to the earliest Old Testament times, so we will begin by looking at what it meant to the ancient people of God. We will see how all this foreshadowed the greatest sacrifice of all, made by Jesus.

Then we will consider how the New Testament applies the theme of sacrifice to the lives of Christians, who are to be 'a holy priesthood, offering spiritual sacrifices acceptable to God through Jesus Christ' (1 Peter 2:5).

Some familiar aspects of the Christian life will be considered – praying, praising, serving, doing good, giving and witnessing. But we will look at them in a particular way, asking how and why the New Testament uses the idea of sacrifice to describe these practices.

For example, Hebrews 13:15 says, 'Through Jesus, therefore, let us continually offer to God a sacrifice of praise – the fruit of lips that openly profess his name.' What new understanding can we gain by looking at praise through the lens of sacrifice? How do the ideas behind the Old Testament sacrificial system relate to praising God today? In the following chapters these and other questions will be considered in connection with the various New Testament verses that speak of sacrifice in the Christian life.

When Jesus called people to follow him, he challenged them to count the cost of discipleship. They needed to know what they were letting themselves in for! Life with Jesus was to be fulfilling but also demanding. The same is true today. Anyone seeking to follow Jesus needs to be aware of the cost of commitment. My hope is that this book will help to make that clearer. It could, therefore, be useful for new Christians wanting to know more about the life of faith and service. It may equally be a helpful refresher for more-experienced followers of Jesus.

The various aspects of sacrifice that are explored may prove challenging. Writing about them has certainly challenged me. But they are part of what it means to be a follower of Jesus, so they need to be considered carefully and prayerfully. That is why each section is followed by a Reflection designed to help you think about what has been written and what it may mean for you personally. That way the contents of the chapters can move beyond theory to inspire thought, commitment and action.

The Reflection pages include Scripture readings and questions to consider. It might be helpful to write your thoughts down. There are no right or wrong answers. The hope is simply that through reflection and prayer you will come to a better understanding of what it means to put yourself – heart, mind and will – 'on the altar'.

Part One

A Picture of Sacrifice

... a holy priesthood, offering spiritual sacrifices acceptable to God through Jesus Christ.
(1 Peter 2:5)

Chapter 1
The Power of Pictures

A PICTURE paints a thousand words. Indeed, pictures are sometimes better because the human mind prefers images to abstract words. The same is true of picture-*language*, which is why good preachers, poets and story-tellers use it all the time.

Jesus used picture-language in his parables to illustrate the Kingdom of God: it is like a mustard seed, like yeast or like treasure hidden in a field (Luke 13:18-21; Matthew 13:31-33, 44). When New Testament writers describe the Church, they use the picture-language of metaphor.

The Church is pictured in various ways:
- as a field in which God makes things grow (1 Corinthians 3:6-9),
- as a temple in which God's Spirit lives (1 Corinthians 3:16-17; Ephesians 2:21-22),
- as a body with different parts working together (1 Corinthians 12:12-27),
- as a flock cared for by shepherds and by God (1 Peter 5:1-4),
- as a bride, loved by Christ and called to be radiant and pure (Ephesians 5:25-27; Revelation 19:7-8).

Individual Christians are also pictured:
- as athletes who need to train with discipline and run with determination to win the eternal prize (1 Corinthians 9:24-27; Hebrews 12:1-3),
- as soldiers who are single-minded and well-equipped for battle (2 Timothy 2:3-4; Ephesians 6:10-17).

Sacrifice is one of the most significant images in the New Testament, but before we begin to explore it, let us think a little more about metaphors and how they work.

The power of metaphor

Metaphors are images from one area of life applied to another area of life so that we can understand it better. By making connections and comparisons between things that are not usually connected, new and helpful insights are possible. Metaphors throw light on a situation and help us to see it more clearly.

For example, when we speak of 'a roller-coaster of emotions' we are using an image from a fairground to describe what happens to someone's feelings. It is a vivid way of describing fluctuating – and sometimes extreme – emotional experiences that can be caused by sudden changes in circumstances.

In the same way, biblical metaphors apply familiar images to life in order to aid our understanding. When Paul portrays the Christian as a soldier in the sixth chapter of Ephesians, he helps us think about what it means to be involved in a spiritual battle. We see the challenge of being a Christian (the fight) and at the same time we are made aware of the resources available to us (the armour of God).

The potential of metaphor

So metaphors help us *see* life. And they can also *shape* life – or at least shape our responses to it.

This has happened in the world of science. When 17th-century scientists began imagining the universe as a machine created by God, they were using a metaphor that not only helped them understand the universe as they knew it but which also gave them insights that advanced their understanding.

Like a machine, the universe was understood to work according to fixed principles – not in a haphazard way, but reliably and predictably. As a result, dependable theories could be formed and these became the foundation of scientific and technological progress for a further three centuries.

Metaphors can also shape the spiritual life. For example, picturing the Christian as a soldier of Christ helps to create a certain attitude and approach to mission. It fosters dedication, endurance and a sense of purpose – and it opens up new possibilities. When William Booth renamed The Christian Mission as The Salvation Army in 1878, he was not only describing what the movement had become – because military terminology and organisation had already been introduced by then – but he was also opening up a whole new range of imaginative possibilities for how the movement could develop and what its members might do. Even *he* had no idea how significant that new name was to be.

The military metaphor helped to revolutionise the work and heralded its dramatic expansion. What had been a small mission, working mainly in London, grew rapidly to become an international Army of devoted soldiers determined to win the world for Jesus!

The significance of sacrifice
Peter described the Church as 'a holy priesthood, offering spiritual sacrifices acceptable to God through Jesus Christ' (1 Peter 2:5). This means that, just as priests offered sacrifices to God as part of Jewish worship, so Christians offer spiritual sacrifices as their response to God.

Peter used a metaphor that was deeply significant for his readers. The Old Testament sacrificial system was familiar to the earliest Christians because sacrifice was still practised by Jews in New Testament times until the destruction of Jerusalem by the Romans in AD 70. If a picture paints a thousand words, this picture spoke volumes to the early believers who were beginning to understand their new-found faith.

The idea of sacrifice is not so familiar to us. When we look at Jewish sacrificial practices we enter what feels like a strange and confusing world – a world of priests, rituals, altars and burnt offerings. So before we begin to explore the metaphor of sacrifice we need to gain a clearer understanding of the Old Testament practice.

Chapter 2
Orders and Regulations for Sacrifices

THE Book of Leviticus sets out Moses' orders and regulations for sacrifices. These were focused on the tabernacle – or tent of meeting – which symbolised God's presence with the people, first in the desert, then in the Promised Land. Later, the tabernacle would be replaced by the Temple in Jerusalem. Leviticus, along with other parts of the Old Testament, shows why sacrifices were offered, what kinds there were, and how and when they took place.

Why were sacrifices made?
Leviticus begins with the words, 'The Lord called to Moses and spoke to him from the tent of meeting'. So Moses' orders and regulations for sacrifices were actually God's ordinances. They expressed his desire to meet with his people and were a means of making it possible.

Although sacrifices could be made for various reasons, such as dedication, thanksgiving or fellowship, atonement was always the underlying purpose. The sins of the people separated them from God, but sacrifices made atonement for their sins and brought the people back to him. Sacrifices were a vivid reminder that sin disrupted their relationship with God and that something had to be offered in order to restore it.

The shedding of blood was significant because, as the source and symbol of life, it was regarded as sacred. When blood was shed and life was given up in death, it was done on behalf of, or in the place of, the worshippers. In this way atonement was made for their sins: 'It is the blood that makes atonement for one's life' (Leviticus 17:11).

The sacrifices themselves could not deal with the problem of sin because they had no inherent power to create forgiveness. It was simply that God, in his mercy, chose them as the means of bringing his people back to himself.

An animal sacrifice could be a bull, a sheep or a goat, although poor people were permitted to offer two turtle-doves or pigeons. Only domestic animals could be offered because the sacrifice had to involve giving up and giving to God something that belonged to them. Wild animals could not be offered because, by definition, the people did not own them. And the animals had to be without defect because only the best was good enough for God.

There were also non-animal sacrifices of grain, flour, oils, wine and incense. These were all produced by human effort; as such, they belonged to the people and could therefore be given up in sacrifice.

What kinds of sacrifices were there?

The burnt offering (Leviticus 1)
This was the earliest and most common kind of sacrifice. Its purpose was to make atonement for sins. The Hebrew word for burnt offering literally means 'that which goes up'. Unlike other sacrifices, the complete animal was burnt, symbolising that the offering was wholly for God. Because the sacrifice represented the worshipper, the emphasis was on the complete dedication of the worshipper to God.

So first came atonement and then came dedication. The burnt offering was a voluntary sacrifice in which the worshippers acknowledged their sin, claimed God's forgiveness and responded in total commitment to him.

The grain offering (Leviticus 2)
The grain offering accompanied every burnt offering. The grain or flour could be uncooked, with oil and frankincense added. Or it could be mixed with oil and baked as a cake. A drink offering of wine was usually given with the grain offering. All these ingredients were natural but were also cultivated by human hands. The offering therefore represented the people's thanksgiving for God's provision and the dedication of their daily work to him.

The fellowship offering (Leviticus 3)
This sacrifice celebrated peace and harmony. The fat of the animal was placed on the embers of the burnt offering and the rest was eaten by the people. On the basis of the atonement gained through the burnt

offering, and following the dedication of daily work in the grain offering, the people could feast together in friendship with one another and fellowship with God.

The sin offering (Leviticus 4:1 to 5:13)
The burnt offering provided atonement for deliberate and conscious sins, but some sins could be committed unintentionally – mostly in connection with ritual practices. For example, the people were required to obey strict rules of ceremonial cleanliness, such as not touching the carcass of an unclean animal. These rules could be broken accidentally, so once they realised they had committed such sins, the sacrifice was to be made and they were then purified.

The guilt offering (Leviticus 5:14 to 6:7)
The guilt offering included the important element of restitution, and so was mostly for cases in which a loss could be assessed financially. Before the sacrifice was made, compensation had to be paid to the person who had been sinned against, whether intentionally or unintentionally. Significantly, Leviticus recognises that a sin against another person is also a sin against God.

How were sacrifices carried out?
From these early chapters of Leviticus we can piece together a general picture of how sacrifices were to be carried out. First, the worshipper brought the offering to the place of sacrifice. This was near the altar, rather than on the altar itself.

Next, the worshipper laid his hand on the head of the animal. Usually he would confess his sins, which were symbolically transferred to the animal so that it represented the worshipper's sinfulness.

The animal was then killed, either by the worshipper himself or, on national occasions, by a priest. A priest would then collect the blood of the animal in a basin and splash it against the northeast and southwest corners of the altar so that it covered all four sides.

Next came the full or partial burning of the sacrifice on the altar to signify that it was given to God.

Finally, except when the sacrifice was completely destroyed, what was left over was eaten.

When were sacrifices offered?
Private and individual sacrifices could be offered at various times, but public sacrifices took place at set times. There were twice-daily offerings (in the morning and the evening) and there were Sabbath offerings.

The Sabbath was the highlight of the week. It was a day 'to the LORD' (Exodus 20:10) and a day of rest which involved sacrifices and feasting. A number of annual occasions also included sacrifice. The most important was the Day of Atonement.

The Day of Atonement (Leviticus 16)
This communal occasion brought the people of Israel together in recognition of God's holiness and their unworthiness. It was a day of penitence, which was expressed through fasting, and a day when atonement was made for all the sins of the people. The high priest would sacrifice a bull for himself and his household, and a goat for the sins of the people. He would take the blood into the Most Holy Place (the Holy of Holies) within the tabernacle and sprinkle it on the atonement cover (or mercy seat) that lay on the Ark of the Covenant.

The final act involved a second goat, the scapegoat. With his hands on the scapegoat's head, the high priest would confess the sins of the people so that they were transferred to the animal. It was then sent into the desert as a symbol of sin being carried away.

Other annual festivals
Three other annual sacrificial events took place. These were pilgrimage festivals when the entire population travelled to Jerusalem. Unlike the Day of Atonement, which emphasised sorrow and repentance, these were joyful feasts. They highlighted important aspects of the faith of the people of Israel.

The Passover (Deuteronomy 16:1-8)
The Passover commemorated the Exodus from Egypt. Every family was expected to offer a lamb for sacrifice at the Temple. This was to remind them of the lambs that were sacrificed in Egypt. The blood of the lambs had been smeared on the people's door frames so that God's judgment would 'pass over' and they would be spared. The Passover lamb was sacrificed at the Temple in the afternoon and eaten at the Passover meal in the evening.

On the Altar

The Feast of Weeks or Pentecost (Deuteronomy 16:9-12)
This festival took place 50 days after Passover. It celebrated the gathering of the barley harvest, part of which was given as a freewill offering to God. There were also animal sacrifices and a communal feast.

The Feast of Booths (Deuteronomy 16:13-15)
During this festival the people would live for seven days in shelters (booths or tabernacles) made from branches to remind them of the 40 years in the wilderness that followed the Exodus. Animal sacrifices and grain offerings were made each day.

Sacrifice was central to the lives of the people of Israel. The same could be said about people of other nations at that time. But Israel's system was uniquely set within the context of the people's relationship with God. Sadly, the people were not always faithful to that relationship. As we will see in the next chapter, this is where the prophets came in, calling the people back to the God who had created them for a special purpose.

Chapter 3
Prophet and Loss

THE sacrificial system mattered to the people of God because it established and maintained their covenant relationship with him. In this covenant relationship God acted for his people and made promises to them. In return, he expected their obedience. The Old Testament describes various covenants.

The first, made with Noah and his sons after the flood, included all future generations and every living creature. God promised to never again destroy all life on Earth by a flood, and signified this with a rainbow (Genesis 9:8-17).

God then established the patriarchal covenant. It began with Abram being renamed Abraham and consisted primarily of God's promise to give him descendants and a land (Genesis 17).

After God rescued the people from Egypt a covenant was made at Mount Sinai. The previous covenants were made with particular individuals, and extended to their descendants. The Sinai covenant (or Mosaic covenant, named after Moses) was made with the people as a whole. God said:

> You yourselves have seen what I did to Egypt, and how I carried you on eagles' wings and brought you to myself. Now if you obey me fully and keep my covenant, then out of all nations you will be my treasured possession. Although the whole earth is mine, you will be for me a kingdom of priests and a holy nation.
> (Exodus 19:4-6)

The Sinai covenant resulted from God's deliverance of the people from Egypt. It included promises of blessing and required obedience to the Ten Commandments and to numerous other regulations.

Generations later, the Davidic covenant developed the Sinai covenant. It was needed because the king had become the mediator between God and the people, and it was primarily a promise to David that his descendants would reign for ever (2 Samuel 7).

These different covenants were connected. All were initiated by God and formed of his promises. Each added something to the previous one as new situations developed, so they can be thought of as related parts of an ongoing covenant relationship between God and his people.

Later still, the prophet Jeremiah spoke of a 'new covenant' between God and the people in which 'the law' would be 'in their minds' and 'on their hearts', and by which their sins would be forgiven (Jeremiah 31:31-34). This is the covenant that Jesus established with the offering of his life (Matthew 26:27-28; 1 Corinthians 11:25-26).

Called to be different

The Sinai covenant meant that Israel was to be distinct from other nations. As a 'holy nation' it was special to God and was to reflect his holiness. But this was a tall order, so there had to be a way of reminding the people of the need for holiness. And they required a means to renew their relationship with God when they failed. Sacrifice was the means God provided to maintain the covenant relationship. It enabled the people to fulfil their calling to be different.

Unfortunately, the reality of sacrificial practice did not always live up to the high ideals set out by Moses. Over time other influences crept in from the religions of neighbouring nations, as well as from the religions that had dominated Canaan before the people of Israel arrived. Certain prophets called the people's attention to the problem. At first glance they seem to be passionately opposed to sacrifice. Here, for example, is Amos speaking for God:

> I hate, I despise your religious festivals; your assemblies are a stench to me. Even though you bring me burnt offerings and grain offerings, I will not accept them. Though you bring choice fellowship offerings, I will have no regard for them.
>
> (Amos 5:21-22)

God appears to have gone off the idea of sacrifice! However, looking more closely we see that the issue was not sacrifice itself, but the way that it was being abused. Sacrifice was meant to be a heartfelt response to the covenant grace of God but, under the influence of other religions, it came to be seen as a way of manipulating God – an almost magical ritual to gain God's favour so that fields and people would be fertile.

Sacrifice was intended to be just part of the people's overall response to God. Concern for others was also required – not just hearts to God, but also hands to people. Instead, worship became separated from lifestyle so that corruption, indifference and injustice were common. Here is Isaiah's verdict:

> See how the faithful city has become a prostitute! She once was full of justice; righteousness used to dwell in her – but now murderers! Your silver has become dross, your choice wine is diluted with water. Your rulers are rebels, partners with thieves; they all love bribes and chase after gifts. They do not defend the cause of the fatherless; the widow's case does not come before them.
>
> (Isaiah 1:21-23)

Called back to obedience

According to the prophets, something had been lost. What was good had gone bad, what was fruitful had turned rotten. Jeremiah pointed out that they had stopped listening to God and obeying him:

> This is what the LORD Almighty, the God of Israel, says: go ahead, add your burnt offerings to your other sacrifices and eat the meat yourselves! For when I brought your ancestors out of Egypt and spoke to them, I did not just give them commands about burnt offerings and sacrifices, but I gave them this command: obey me, and I will be your God and you will be my people. Walk in obedience to all I command you, that it may go well with you. But they did not listen or pay attention; instead, they followed the stubborn inclinations of their evil hearts. They went backwards and not forwards.
>
> (Jeremiah 7:21-24)

Because of this the people's sacrifices had become unacceptable to God. There was a way back though. They were to become obedient to him once more. Micah spelt it out clearly and simply:

> And what does the LORD require of you? To act justly and to love mercy and to walk humbly with your God.
>
> (Micah 6:8)

On the Altar

The prophets were calling people back to the original ideals of the covenant outlined by Moses. He had been both prophet and priest. As a prophet Moses called the people to be holy because God was holy. It was a holiness that involved obedience to God in matters of personal morality and social justice. As a priest Moses assured the people that when they failed to live up to these high standards – as they surely would – there was a way back to fellowship with God through the system of sacrifices.

But performing a ritual was not enough by itself. Repentance, heartfelt devotion and a sincere concern for others were also required. This was the message of the prophets as they tried to regain what had been lost.

Chapter 4
A Living Metaphor

WHEN Peter described Christians as 'a holy priesthood, offering spiritual sacrifices' (1 Peter 2:5), he was picturing Old Testament sacrifices. These were still practised in his day and he saw them as a metaphor for the Christian life. We discovered earlier that metaphors can open up new and helpful insights. This is true with the picture of sacrifice. When the New Testament uses this image in connection with aspects of the Christian life it brings out fresh meanings. And even though the sacrificial system comes from an ancient world and might not seem relevant today, the metaphor is alive and meaningful for us.

A number of significant themes connected with Old Testament sacrifice will appear again and again as we explore the New Testament metaphor in later chapters. They concern grace, obedience, costliness, restoration and integration.

A foundation of grace
We tend to think of grace as a New Testament concept but it is also the foundation of God's relationship with his people in the Old Testament. When Moses encountered God, he heard words of grace:

> And he passed in front of Moses, proclaiming, 'The LORD, the LORD, the compassionate and gracious God, slow to anger, abounding in love and faithfulness …'
> (Exodus 34:6)

Grace is God's undeserved favour towards people. Such grace was expressed in the sacrificial system, which was a God-given solution to the problem of sin and separation. It was not the people's idea, it was not even Moses' idea. Moses received these orders and regulations from God. The sacrificial system was a gift of grace that enabled the covenant relationship between God and the people to be maintained. And the covenant itself was a relationship of grace, based on the compassion of God who delivered the people from Egypt and promised them his blessing.

An obedient response
The God who called the people out of Egypt and into a covenant relationship expected his people to live in obedience to his commands. The sacrificial system was an expression of this obedience. God commanded the people to offer sacrifices and he set out in detail the way in which they were to be done.

But sacrifices were more than acts of obedience. They were also an indication of the importance of obedience. So highly did God value the people's obedience in matters of personal morality and social justice, that only through sacrifice could their disobedience be atoned for and their relationship with him be maintained. Sacrifice demonstrated that obedience mattered.

A costly gift
Sacrifices were costly. As we have seen, the sacrificial animal was domestic rather than wild. It was the property of the worshipper, so there was a cost in offering it. Not only that, but the animal had to be without defect – the best of the bunch. A sacrifice was a real sacrifice!

The cost of sacrifice was also expressed in non-animal offerings such as grain, oil and wine. These had been produced by human effort, so by offering them they were giving to God not only the food but the work involved in producing it.

Sacrifices represented the people's costly commitment to God in response to his gracious commitment to them.

A restored relationship
Sacrifice was a means of restoring the people's fellowship with God. By sacrifice the people were purified from the sins that had separated them from God. They were free to make a clean start.

As noted in Chapter Two, sacrifice in itself had no power to do this. Forgiveness and restoration did not come through a ritual but by the grace of God. Nevertheless, sacrifice was a significant act because it gave the assurance that God would do what the act symbolised. What was important was not the ritual itself, but the people's relationship with God. Sacrifice was both an expression of the relationship (because it was done in obedience to God) and also a means to maintain it (because it symbolised forgiveness and restoration).

An integrated life

The prophets reminded the people that sacrifice should not be isolated from the rest of their lives. What mattered to God was not just their worship, but their everyday behaviour. If they were disobeying God by living sinfully and by mistreating others, their sacrifices were of no use at all. Every aspect of their lives was to be an expression of their covenant relationship with God. Prayer, sacrifice, personal morality, kindness and social justice were to be combined into one integrated response to God's grace. They were to live joined-up lives.

These themes, which are associated with Old Testament sacrifice, take on a richer and deeper meaning when we come to the New Testament. They are at the heart of Christian spirituality and living – and it is often the metaphor of sacrifice that is used to emphasise their importance.

But before we start looking at these, we need to pause and consider the most important sacrifice of all – the sacrifice of Jesus.

Chapter 5
The Sacrifice of Jesus

THE New Testament uses a variety of metaphors to describe the death of Jesus and how it makes atonement for us, bringing us into a right relationship with God. Three of these appear together in one passage:

> There is no difference between Jew and Gentile, for all have sinned and fall short of the glory of God, and all are **justified** freely by his grace through the **redemption** that came by Christ Jesus. God presented Christ as a **sacrifice** of atonement, through the shedding of his blood – to be received by faith.
>
> (Romans 3:22-25)

These three pictures of the Atonement are drawn from the law court (justification), the slave market (redemption) and the Temple (sacrifice). The reason Paul uses such pictures is that the truth of Jesus' achievement on the Cross is so far beyond our understanding that we can only begin to grasp it by means of images. These metaphors, along with others in the New Testament, provide different but complementary aspects of the meaning of the Atonement. All the metaphors are important, but the image of sacrifice dominates New Testament teaching about the death of Jesus. This is not surprising. Early Jewish Christians were so familiar with the practice of sacrifice that they naturally saw the death of Jesus in this way. As Paul Fiddes says:

> When Christian believers reflected upon their experience of being restored to fellowship with God through the death of Jesus, the idea of sacrifice was immediately illuminating. 'It's just like a sacrifice,' they said.[2]

Acts 6:7 states, 'So the word of God spread. The number of disciples in Jerusalem increased rapidly,' then adds the comment, 'and a large number of priests became obedient to the faith'. This remark, easily overlooked, gives a telling insight into the power of the metaphor of sacrifice. Priests administered the sacrificial system. So, when the death of Jesus was portrayed as a sacrifice, they would see the connection with the rituals they were performing and understand the meaning of the gospel more clearly. No wonder 'a large number' came to faith.

The metaphor of sacrifice is rich and meaningful. It helps us understand the death of Jesus. Although the picture comes to us from another time it still stirs hearts, inspires minds and motivates commitment today.

A full and final sacrifice

The crucifixion of Jesus is portrayed as the fulfilment of Old Testament sacrifices. Those sacrifices foreshadowed the reality of the atonement that was provided through his death. The sacrificial system was only a limited and temporary measure, designed to cover the people's sins and enable them to maintain their covenant relationship with God. The sacrifice of Jesus was full and final.

> Day after day every priest stands and performs his religious duties; again and again he offers the same sacrifices, which can never take away sins. But when this priest had offered for all time one sacrifice for sins, he sat down at the right hand of God.
> (Hebrews 10:11-12)

The blood of animals could not atone for sin, but the death of Jesus did. His sacrifice provided atonement, potentially, for the whole human race, and ended the need for animal sacrifices.

The language of metaphor

At the same time it is important to remember that when we think of the death of Jesus as a sacrifice, we are still using picture-language.

It is not a literal sacrifice in the way that Old Testament animals were sacrificed. It is a metaphor in which aspects of the Old Testament ritual are used, and sometimes spiritualised, to describe the death of Jesus and what it achieved. For example, in Romans 3:25 the original Greek text describes Jesus as a *hilastērion*, which can refer to the golden cover (or mercy seat) of the Ark of the Covenant – the place where the blood of the sacrifice was sprinkled on the Day of Atonement. And when Jesus is described as 'a lamb without blemish or defect' (1 Peter 1:19) it refers to his spiritual and moral perfection.

Obviously Jesus is not literally a golden cover or a lamb. Metaphors are at work, pointing to a deeper significance.

Pictures of sacrifice

The picture of sacrifice is used in various ways in connection with the Atonement. Sometimes the death of Jesus is seen as a particular kind of sacrifice. For example, 1 Corinthians 5:7 states, 'Christ, our Passover lamb, has been sacrificed' and in Hebrews the image is of the Day of Atonement: 'He did not enter by means of the blood of goats and calves; but he entered the Most Holy Place once for all by his own blood' (9:12). Often the image is less specific, such as when Jesus is referred to as 'the Lamb of God' (John 1:29) or 'a fragrant offering and sacrifice to God' (Ephesians 5:2).

The metaphor of sacrifice is used to describe, not only the death of Jesus, but also what his death achieved. So John's first epistle informs us that 'the blood of Jesus, his Son, purifies us from all sin' (1 John 1:7) and Hebrews, recalling the Day of Atonement, declares:

> How much more, then, will the blood of Christ, who through the eternal Spirit offered himself unblemished to God, cleanse our consciences from acts that lead to death, so that we may serve the living God!
>
> (9:14)

In using such imagery, the New Testament writers echo the thoughts of the Old Testament prophet Isaiah when he described the servant of God in Isaiah 53. This servant was 'an offering for sin', who 'took up our pain and bore our suffering', was 'pierced for our transgressions' and 'crushed for our iniquities'. His was 'the punishment that brought us peace'. And 'by his wounds we are healed' because 'the Lord has laid on him the iniquity of us all'. The early Christians saw these words as clear references to Jesus.

Another of the interesting and moving aspects of the picture of sacrifice in Hebrews is that, not only is Jesus the sacrifice, he is also the high priest who offers himself as the sacrifice: 'He sacrificed for their sins once for all when he offered himself' (7:27).

It is a vivid picture of the self-giving of Jesus. We are not to see the Atonement as God punishing an innocent victim. Rather, it is God, in Christ, offering himself as a sacrifice and taking upon himself the sins of the world.

The Kingdom of God
The focus so far has been on the sacrifice of Jesus as the means of restoring humanity's relationship with God. But the New Testament has a larger vision than that.

To begin with, the death of Jesus should not be seen in isolation from his birth, life, teaching, resurrection, ascension and future return. All these events are part of his mission to establish God's reign on Earth, the Kingdom of God. And when we become the kind of living sacrifice described in the rest of this book we are joining in this work by experiencing the reign of God in our lives and extending the reign of God in the world around us.

Another important point to understand is that the sacrifice of Jesus, as part of his complete work, has power to transform the whole of creation. Yes, it removes the pollution of sin from our lives but that is just part of the greater purpose to remove evil from the created order and to renew it. This is what Paul means when he says, 'The creation itself will be liberated from its bondage to decay and brought into the freedom and glory of the children of God' (Romans 8:21).

These two purposes are linked again in Ephesians 1:7-10 where Paul speaks of personal salvation, which is 'redemption through his blood, the forgiveness of sins', and of cosmic salvation, 'which he purposed in Christ, to be put into effect when the times reach their fulfilment – to bring unity to all things in heaven and on earth under Christ'.

The bigger picture
Two important things have been said about the relationship between the sacrifice of Jesus and the sacrifices of the Old Testament. The first is that the New Testament takes the Old Testament practice and uses it as a metaphor for the death of Jesus. Sacrifice is a picture of what Jesus did and what it means for us.

But we have also seen that the sacrifice of Jesus was the fulfilment of the Old Testament rituals. They foreshadowed the reality that came with him. Their achievements were limited and temporary – his was full and final. So, although it is true to say that sacrifice is a picture of what Jesus did on the Cross, we need also to say that in some sense it really was a sacrifice. It involved real giving, real obedience, real cost and achieved a real reconciliation with God.

More than that – the sacrifice of Jesus reveals a bigger picture. An intriguing verse in Revelation refers to Jesus as 'the Lamb who was slain from the creation of the world' (13:8). This tells us that the sacrifice of Jesus, as an event in history, was the expression of what God is like in eternity – self-giving and self-sacrificing. It is this God who called the people of Israel to himself, who provided the sacrificial system to maintain their covenant relationship with him and who gave himself in Christ for the salvation of the world.

In the chapters that follow we will see how Old Testament sacrificial imagery is used in the New Testament to describe the life of faith. But in doing this we cannot overlook the sacrifice of Jesus. Although his sacrifice is not referred to explicitly in these sacrificial images of Christian living, it is there as the backdrop that gives context and meaning to all we do.

Reflection One

The Sacrifice of Jesus

Jesus is at the centre of human history. His birth, life, death and resurrection are events that illuminate all that preceded them and they have had an impact on everything that has unfolded since.

- *How does your understanding of the death of Jesus change as you look at it through the lens of sacrifice in the Old Testament? Is there a positive impact or not?*

The prophet Isaiah wrote a beautiful description of a suffering servant whose destiny was to be a sacrifice as 'the LORD has laid on him the iniquity of us all'.

Read Isaiah 52:13-15 and 53:1-12.

- *What parallels do you find in the life of Jesus with the description of the one called the 'man of sorrows' in Isaiah 53:3 (King James Version)?*

Very soon after the Crucifixion, the New Testament writers define the central tenets of the Christian faith. The shameful death of Jesus is transformed into the glorious means of forgiveness and salvation.

It is not an isolated, random event but one which fulfils God's eternal plan to redeem the world:

> For what I received I passed on to you as of first importance: that Christ died for our sins according to the Scriptures…
> (1 Corinthians 15:3)

- *Think about how you first heard of the meaning of the sacrifice of Jesus. Is there a particular person who comes to mind? Which other people have helped you and taught you to grow in your faith?*

- *Offer a prayer of thanks to God for those people and ask him to equip you to pass on the gospel message to others.*

Read Philippians 2:5-11.

These verses suggest that the sacrifice of Jesus encompasses much more than the particular event of his death on the Cross. His entire life expresses his humility, obedience and willingness to serve.

He sacrificed equality with God for life on Earth with all that it meant to be fully human.

- *As you read these verses consider the opening line:*
  'The attitude you should have is the one that Christ Jesus had.'
  (Philippians 2:5 Good News Bible)

- *What particular challenge does that bring you? What might need to change in you? In the pattern of your life?*

Charles Wesley wrote:

> Amazing love! how can it be
> That thou, my God, shouldst die for me?
> *(SASB 241 v 1)*

Wesley's response is one of amazement and incredulity that God himself came to Earth to be our Saviour.

- *Take this as your starting point for prayer as you bring before God all you have received through reflecting on the sacrifice of Jesus.*

Part Two

A Living Sacrifice

*… offer your bodies as a living
sacrifice, holy and pleasing to God
– this is your true and proper worship.
(Romans 12:1)*

Chapter 6
Total Dedication

BISHOP John Taylor Smith was honorary chaplain to Queen Victoria and a popular speaker at the annual Keswick Convention in England. A later Keswick speaker remembered: 'It was Bishop Taylor Smith who used to say that every morning when he woke up, he lay for a moment and in that moment turned his bed into an altar and offered himself afresh to God.'³ As he did this the good bishop might have been thinking of Romans 12:1, where Paul urges his readers to offer their bodies as a living sacrifice.

As we saw in Chapter Two, the Old Testament sacrificial system had various kinds of sacrifice. Only one kind, the burnt offering, was completely burnt up to show that the offering was wholly for God. This is the idea Paul had in mind – a total dedication of our lives. Nothing kept back, but everything given to God.

This kind of dedication is expressed simply and beautifully in a song by William Himes:

> All that I am, all I can be,
> All that I have, all that is me,
> Accept and use, Lord, as you would choose, Lord,
> Right now today.
> Take ev'ry passion, ev'ry skill,
> Take all my dreams and bend them to your will.
> My all I give, Lord, for you I'll live, Lord,
> Come what may.⁴
>
> (*SASB* 568, chorus)

Being a living sacrifice means giving 'my all' to God. But, as someone once said, 'The trouble with a living sacrifice is that it keeps crawling off the altar!' This highlights the need for an ongoing renewal of our dedication to God. The Christian life begins as we respond to God in repentance, faith and commitment – and while that initial dedication remains vitally important, it needs to be renewed frequently, even daily. Our spiritual experience is one long series of fresh commitments. This was what Bishop Taylor Smith was doing as he turned his bed into an altar each morning.

In view of God's mercy

A word at the beginning of Romans 12 puts our sacrifice into its proper context – it is the word 'therefore'. Paul writes:

> Therefore, I urge you, brothers and sisters, in view of God's mercy, to offer your bodies as a living sacrifice, holy and pleasing to God – this is your true and proper worship.
>
> (Romans 12:1)

The word 'therefore' points back to previous chapters that provide the context, the basis and the motivation for what is to follow. Romans begins with belief (chapters 1-11) and ends with behaviour (chapters 12-16). It moves from creed to conduct. This is not surprising, because what we believe affects what we do. The principles of our faith are worked out in the practices of daily living. This book follows the same pattern. In part one we began with the theory and doctrine of sacrifice – now we are turning to the practical expression of sacrifice in our daily lives.

When Paul says the sacrificial offering of ourselves is 'in view of God's mercy' he is referring specifically to Romans 11:30-32, where he mentions God's mercy to Israel, which now extends to the Gentiles. But Paul has more than these few verses in mind. He is also summarising all the previous chapters in Romans, which highlight the grace and mercy of God. The human race has a problem, 'for all have sinned and fall short of the glory of God' (Romans 3:23). But God has graciously provided the solution:

> All are justified freely by his grace through the redemption that came by Christ Jesus. God presented Christ as a sacrifice of atonement, through the shedding of his blood – to be received by faith.
>
> (Romans 3:24-25)

This is the context of Paul's call for us to offer ourselves as a living sacrifice – the grace and mercy of God shown to us in the sacrificial death of Jesus, which deals with the problem of sin and reconciles us to God. It is important to understand this context. We cannot reconcile ourselves to God. We do not have the ability to do that. It is grace acting on our behalf in Jesus that makes us right with God.

When Paul appeals for us to be a living sacrifice he is not saying that this offering of ourselves is what saves us. Jesus saves us by his sacrificial death. Our offering is the response to this salvation, not the cause of it. Peter agrees. He says our spiritual sacrifices are 'acceptable to God through Jesus Christ' (1 Peter 2:5). Only on the basis of Jesus' saving death is the offering of who we are and what we do presentable to God. And when Paul says our offering is 'pleasing to God', it does not mean that our dedication is good enough to please God and persuade him to accept us. Rather, God is pleased when we respond to all that he has done for us.

Leaping into the light

Some people can be wary of making the kind of dedication that becoming a living sacrifice involves. They may wonder what God will ask them to do, where he will want them to go or what he might expect them to become. It can feel like taking a huge leap into the dark. Catherine Booth felt that way as her husand William left the Methodist ministry to become an itinerant evangelist. She wrote to her mother in 1861:

> At times it appears to me that God may have something very glorious in store for us, and when he has tried us he will bring us forth as gold. It will not be the first time I have taken a leap in the dark, humanly speaking, for conscience' sake! [5]

From a human point of view it appeared to be a leap in the dark, but Catherine's trust in God helped her to look at the situation from a different perspective. She believed God had 'something very glorious in store'. She had expressed this kind of faith before when, as a teenager, she wrote in her journal:

> I know not what he is about to do with me, but I have given myself entirely into his hands.[6]

Although we do not know what the future holds, the one thing we can know is that our commitment is not a leap into the dark, even if it feels that way. We are putting ourselves into the hands of God, so it is a leap into the light!

We have already seen that the call to be a living sacrifice is made in the context of God's grace and mercy. He has committed himself to us in the life, death and resurrection of Jesus. He loves us. This is an amazing reality – one that surely fills us with a sense of awe and wonder. J. B. Phillips captures something of this in his translation of Romans 12:1: 'With eyes wide open to the mercies of God…'

Wide-eyed with wonder we give ourselves in gratitude, in faith and in total dedication to the One who gave himself for us.

Chapter 7
True and Proper Worship

WHAT exactly does Paul urge us to sacrifice? He is obviously making an analogy with the practice of sacrificing an animal to God. But when he says offer your 'bodies' is it just the physical part of ourselves that God wants? That seems highly unlikely. Greek philosophy distinguished sharply between body and soul, seeing the body as evil and the soul trapped within it as divine and immortal. But Hebrew thought regarded body and soul as an inseparable unity.

Paul followed Hebrew thought rather than Greek philosophy, so when he says offer your bodies he means more than simply flesh and blood. He means the whole package. The word 'body' is shorthand for all that we are – the physical and the spiritual. It includes our whole personality – heart, mind and will – and everything we do, think or say. A few chapters earlier Paul wrote:

> Offer yourselves to God as those who have been brought from death to life; and offer every part of yourself to him as an instrument of righteousness.
> (Romans 6:13)

The idea is the same in Romans 12:1. It is not just a part of ourselves that we give to God, it is 'every part'. As a living sacrifice we are to offer everything that is part of our living selves.

Under the Old Testament system, the Temple, the priests and the objects used in worship were all regarded as holy. This meant they were set apart for the service of God. They were dedicated to him and were for his use only. As a living sacrifice we are 'holy and pleasing to God'. Our lives are offered up to God and we are to live for him.

Bringing worship into life
This commitment does not mean we have to separate ourselves from the world around us. It means exactly the opposite. Instead of taking ourselves out of the world, we take God into it. He becomes part of

our everyday lives at home, among friends, at work, school or college. Every decision we make is influenced by our relationship with him. Everywhere we go and everything we say or do is part of the offering of our lives to him.

Paul says that when we offer ourselves as a living sacrifice it is our 'true and proper worship'. The word he uses here for 'worship' is the same as in Romans 9:4 where he refers to 'the temple worship'. That kind of worship was limited to a particular place and particular times. Our true and proper worship, the living sacrifice that we offer, is free from these limitations.

While there are times and places of worship in which Christians gather to express their devotion and to receive God's blessing and guidance, true and proper worship means that the whole of life is offered up to God wherever we are and whatever we are doing.

Eugene Peterson conveys this thought well in his paraphrase of Romans 12:1 in *The Message* Bible:

> Take your everyday, ordinary life – your sleeping, eating, going-to-work, and walking-around life – and place it before God as an offering.

This attitude gives new meaning to all our daily activities. Take our working lives for example. Being a living sacrifice that is holy and pleasing to God, and seeing all of life as our true and proper worship, will mean we do not work simply for the benefit of our employers or their clients or customers. Neither does it mean we just work in order to earn our wages. It means that we work for God – our motivation is to please him.

On the ruined walls of the old Coventry Cathedral is a set of prayer panels linking worship to daily life. Each brief prayer begins with the words, 'Hallowed be thy name…' One plaque says, 'Hallowed be thy name in commerce – God be at my desk and in my trading.'

The same thought is expressed in a song by Will J. Brand:

> In works or office, field or mart,
>   Where our appointments, Lord, may be,
> Grant that with mind and hand and heart
>   We labour as we would for thee.
>
> (*SASB* 657 v3)

The same goes for other areas of our lives. They are all for God. There is no separation between the sacred and the secular parts of our lives – everything can be a sacred offering. Specific times of worship are important but they only have meaning and worth if they are part of a life of worship in which we give ourselves completely to God and live obediently for him. Sunday worship loses its value if it is not part of week-long worship.

Bringing life into worship
It is also true that Sunday worship gains in value when we bring into it the concerns and joys of the rest of the week. Sometimes we treat worship meetings as a way to escape the world. This is understandable. If we have been hurt, confused or saddened by the experiences of life, it can come as a relief to set these problems aside and simply focus on God. But although God should be at the centre of our worship, allowing us to forget our troubles for part of the time and to be 'lost in wonder, love and praise', we also need room to bring our concerns before him. God is interested in us, so he is interested in whatever troubles us. As we bring our problems to him we see them in the light of his loving purposes for us, and we can be strengthened to face them again.

Sunday worship should also be a time when the important matters that concern society and individuals are addressed. Inequality, poverty, greed, war, the environment, prejudice and exploitation – these are just a few of the issues that meet us in the news every day. Sometimes they affect us personally. More often they are issues that others, or society as a whole, are struggling with. When we meet to worship we can learn to understand them from a Christian perspective and be equipped to face and challenge them – or to help others to face them.

If we are to be a living sacrifice, holy and pleasing to God, we cannot live our lives in compartments – some parts for God, other parts for ourselves, our families, our friends or our employers. There should be no sacred/secular divide. If there is, it needs to be broken down by making all of life an act of worship and by bringing all of life into our acts of worship.

Chapter 8
Metamorphosis

WE are to be a living sacrifice. And like any living thing, if it is to stay healthy it needs to develop. This happens with the human body. It does not stay the same. From the moment we are born we begin to grow. Most of the body's tissues undergo continual change as old cells are discarded and new ones take their place. Even our bones are changing. The entire human skeleton is thought to be replaced every ten years. Physically speaking we are being constantly renewed.

Of course, this does not mean our earthly bodies will last for ever, because other processes are at work that wear us out! Nevertheless, the idea of constant physical renewal helps us understand the need for constant spiritual renewal. Paul emphasises this in Romans 12:2 when he says: 'Be transformed by the renewing of your mind.' Not only do we give ourselves to God, we also allow him to change us.

Transformation
The Greek word which is translated 'transformed' in Romans 12:2 (*metamorphoō*) is only used in three other places in the New Testament. In Matthew 17:2 and Mark 9:2 it is translated 'transfigured' and describes the temporary transformation of Jesus. His face shines like the sun and his clothes become white as he reveals the glory of God.

In 2 Corinthians 3:18 *metamorphoō* describes the way Christians are being changed into the likeness of Jesus: '[We] are being transformed into his image with ever-increasing glory, which comes from the Lord, who is the Spirit.'

We use the word 'metamorphosis' to describe the transformation of a caterpillar into a butterfly or a tadpole into a frog. In both cases an amazing change takes place that gives the creature not only a new appearance, but also the ability to do new things – to fly or to hop. The metamorphosis we experience is even more amazing. In some ways our transformation is just as dramatic and awe-inspiring as the transfiguration of Jesus. In that transformation the glory of God was revealed through the Son of God. In our transformation the glory of God is revealed in the daily lives of weak men and women.

The United Kingdom census of 1981 contained a question about people's occupations. One man wrote, 'I'm a sculptor of stone lions.' The next line asked for more information: 'Please describe the nature of your work.' He wrote, 'I chip away all the bits of stone that are not lion.' God wants us to become like him. His work of transformation involves chipping away everything that is not like him until his glory is revealed.

It is this kind of transformation that the 17th-century French monk Brother Lawrence had in mind when he wrote about his prayer times:

> Sometimes I consider myself there as a stone before a carver, whereof he is to make a statue; presenting myself thus before God, I desire him to form his perfect image in my soul, and make me entirely like himself. [7]

Renewing of the mind
God does not make us more like Jesus by controlling our behaviour as if we were puppets on a string. He works from the inside out! The Holy Spirit refines and purifies our motives, attitudes and aspirations – and this affects the way we act and speak.

That is what Paul means when he says 'be transformed by the renewing of your mind'. An anonymous proverb, which was popular in 19th-century literature, states:

> Sow a thought, and you reap an act;
> Sow an act, and you reap a habit;
> Sow a habit, and you reap a character;
> Sow a character, and you reap a destiny.

The proverb illustrates the power of our thoughts. The mind has a powerful effect on our behaviour and can ultimately determine our destiny. What goes into the mind informs our intellect, influences our attitudes and feeds our imaginations. All this can affect how we feel and what we do.

Of course the influence can go in the other direction as well. How we feel can have an impact on the way we think and the way we act.

And what we do and feel can affect what we think. But it is the power of the mind that concerns Paul. He recognises this power when he says:

> Whatever is true, whatever is noble, whatever is right, whatever is pure, whatever is lovely, whatever is admirable – if anything is excellent or praiseworthy – think about such things.
>
> (Philippians 4:8)

Or as the *Good News Bible* puts it: 'Fill your minds with those things that are good'. He advises this because the contents of our minds – our motives, attitudes and aspirations – really do matter. They have a power over us, for good or for bad.

Renewal of the mind begins when we first become Christians. Part of the conversion experience is repentance. The New Testament Greek word for this is *metanoia*, which according to Archbishop George Carey means 'to think again, to have second thoughts and hence, by implication – to change direction'. [8]

A change of mind leads to a change of life and a new direction. So, renewal of the mind starts with repentance. And as it continues throughout our Christian lives we are transformed more and more into the likeness of Jesus.

Chapter 9
The Word and the Spirit

THE agent of change in renewing our minds is the Holy Spirit. One way the Spirit works is through the Bible, the word of God, which is 'God-breathed and is useful for teaching, rebuking, correcting and training in righteousness, so that the servant of God may be thoroughly equipped for every good work' (2 Timothy 3:16-17).

The Bible has been inspired by the Holy Spirit and the Spirit brings its words to life in our minds. As we read it, study it and allow our minds to be shaped by it, our attitudes and actions can be transformed. We grow in our understanding of what Paul calls God's 'good, pleasing and perfect will' (Romans 12:2) – and we are empowered to do it.

Contemplating his glory

In 2 Corinthians 3:18 Paul writes that we are transformed into the image of Jesus as we 'contemplate' the Lord's glory. The *Amplified Bible* spells it out more clearly, saying we are 'constantly being transfigured' because we 'behold [in the word of God] as in a mirror the glory of the Lord'. [9]

This suggests we need to spend time with God's word. When we look in the mirror in the morning most of us do not just take a quick glance then get on with the rest of our day. We have a good look at ourselves and take time doing what we need to do to appear our best for the day ahead. In the same way we need to take time to see – to behold, to contemplate – what God is saying to us in his word. Only then will it begin to transform us by renewing our minds. We will think more about this in Chapter 13, which is about listening to God.

The Spirit of God works through the word of God but also has a direct influence on our inner lives. The Spirit enters our lives when we first come to faith in Christ. The salvation experience involves repentance, faith and new birth by the Spirit. From that moment, the work of transformation begins as the Spirit starts to make us more like

Jesus by the renewing of our minds. When we offer ourselves to God as a living sacrifice – and as we continue to offer ourselves – we allow the Spirit of God to take control of our lives.

Filled with the Spirit
The New Testament describes this as being 'filled' with the Spirit. When Paul says 'be filled with the Spirit' he is contrasting the experience with being 'drunk on wine', which he condemns (Ephesians 5:18).

To be drunk is to be under the influence of alcohol. To be filled with the Spirit is to be under the influence of the Holy Spirit. The effects are completely different. When the Spirit fills us he influences and empowers us to live like Jesus.

Paul describes the experience using a different image when he refers to the fruit of the Spirit in Galatians 5. Being filled with the Spirit means we 'live by the Spirit' (vv 16 and 25), 'are led by the Spirit' (v 18) and must 'keep in step with the Spirit' (v 25). As a result, the fruit of the Spirit grows in our lives: love, joy, peace, forbearance, kindness, goodness, faithfulness, gentleness and self-control (vv 22-23). These characteristics, which reflect the nature of Jesus, are produced in our lives when we allow his Spirit to fill us and renew our minds.

Just as we need to continually renew our commitment to God and place ourselves on the altar daily, so we need to continually receive the infilling of the Spirit. When Paul says 'be filled with the Spirit' he uses the present tense, which means it is a continuous action. Some versions of the Bible therefore translate Ephesians 5:18 as 'keep on being filled with the Spirit'.[10] It is not a one-off experience, it is a continuous process. We must continually submit to the Spirit's control and receive his grace and power to renew our minds and transform our lives.

Hidden depths
The mind is a complicated thing. There are hidden depths that we cannot understand, let alone control. Psychologists speak of the subconscious mind and the unconscious mind where unknown impulses and instincts exist. These can influence our behaviour without our realising it. This hidden part of the mind seems to have a mind of its own! Memories of bad experiences can sink deep into the mind and become the cause of negative moods and anxieties that affect the way

we act, or react, in certain situations. Such behaviour can be out of character, catching us – and others – by surprise.

Can the word and the Spirit renew these dark corners of our minds? William Sangster, the 20th-century Methodist preacher and holiness teacher, believed they could. He wrote:

> Whatever lies in the sub-conscious capable of rising to consciousness and inciting the will to evil, can rise also to consciousness to be defeated by the willingly received grace of God. So – if a mechanical metaphor may not seem too absurd in this connection – one can imagine a rotary movement of the mind in which desires and impulses clamour to consciousness only to meet the cooling, cleansing breath of God and sink away again to carry health and purity to whatever level of our mental life becomes their home. [11]

We cannot change the hidden depths of our minds, but God can. As we allow the word and the Spirit to influence and inspire us we can be transformed by the renewing of our minds.

The prayer of Leslie Taylor-Hunt can become a reality:

> Give me a holy life, spotless and free,
> Cleansed by the crystal flow coming from thee.
> > Purge the dark halls of thought,
> > Here let thy work be wrought,
> > Each wish and feeling brought
> Captive to thee.
>
> (*SASB* 704 v 1)

—— *Reflection Two* ——
Dedication

- *How have your life experiences thus far shaped your personal view of dedication? Before reading further, take a moment to think about and write down what dedication means for you.*

- *Now consider: Do any of the following scenarios strike a chord with your life just now?*

Do you view 'total dedication' to God as the exclusive prerogative of men and women who are ministers of religion or members of a religious order?

Do you view dedication as a way of life which focuses on developing a particular skill – for example, a young person in training to be an Olympic swimmer? The normal pattern of life will be very different from that of their peers, in the hope that their sacrifice will lead to success and reward.

Do you have a negative view of dedication because you are affected by a person who spends every available moment dedicated to their work or other commitments, while family relationships and responsibilities are neglected?

Do you just feel unable to sustain the kind of dedication you have read about in Part Two – the response to God's grace that involves offering all that you are and have and do?

Or has your whole life been based on commitment to God and constantly renewed dedication to him, but you don't want to become complacent?

- *Bring your thoughts about dedication before God in prayer, both the positive and negative aspects, and receive his loving acceptance.*

We can be assured of this loving acceptance because God himself asks us to place all that we are on the altar. The people of God in the Old Testament were instructed to be selective, to bring animals without blemish, the first fruits and the choicest offerings. There is a good principle at work here, that only the best is good enough for God. However, we will never be 'good enough' by our own efforts, nor can we hide our faults and failings from him. Yet as we read in Romans 12:1 in *The Message*, when we place our 'everyday, ordinary life', our 'sleeping, eating, going-to-work and walking-around life' into God's hands then his Holy Spirit transforms us from the inside out.

- *Conclude this time of reflection by reading Psalm 139. Take time to read it as a personal prayer to the Lord, affirming your desire to dedicate yourself to him and asking him to equip you in the particular challenges you face.*

(It is right to be angry at injustice, but the response in Psalm 139:19-22 hardly seems appropriate. The psalmist fails to distinguish between the sin and the sinner. The verses show, however, that we can voice all our emotions to God; even those that, on reflection, we would regard as unworthy. – Ed.)

Part Three

Praying

*Your prayers and gifts to the poor
have come up as a memorial offering
before God.
(Acts 10:4)*

Chapter 10
The Offering of Prayer

IN New Testament times there was a group of people known as 'God-fearers'. They were Gentiles who had not fully converted to Judaism but who adopted Jewish practices such as prayer and giving to the poor. A Roman centurion named Cornelius was one of them. Acts 10:2 records: 'He and all his family were devout and God-fearing; he gave generously to those in need and prayed to God regularly.'

The verses that follow tell of Cornelius's vision of an angel who described his prayers as 'a memorial offering before God' (Acts 10:4). The memorial offering was part of the grain offering mentioned in Leviticus. It was the part that was burnt before the rest was eaten by the priests. 'The priest shall take a handful of the flour and oil, together with all the incense, and burn this as a memorial portion on the altar, a food offering, an aroma pleasing to the LORD' (Leviticus 2:2). The angel was saying that Cornelius's prayers were like sacrifices to God.

The idea of prayer as a sacrifice was not new. The psalmist had expressed it hundreds of years earlier: 'May my prayer be set before you like incense; may the lifting up of my hands be like the evening sacrifice' (Psalm 141:2). And the image of sacrificial incense is repeated in the final book of the New Testament where John sees the 24 elders worshipping the Lamb of God: 'Each one had a harp and they were holding golden bowls full of incense, which are the prayers of God's people' (Revelation 5:8).

Look out! God at work!
In Cornelius's vision the angel told him to send for Peter. Cornelius was in Caesarea and Peter was in Joppa, about 30 miles away, so it was not until the next day that the messengers arrived at Peter's house. As they approached Joppa, Peter too had a vision.

He saw a large sheet being lowered from Heaven containing all kinds of animals that were ceremonially unclean to the Jews. Then he heard a voice telling him to eat the animals. Peter protested, saying he had never eaten anything that was ceremonially unclean.

The voice said, 'Do not call anything impure that God has made clean' (Acts 10:15). Peter was not sure what all this meant until he went with the messengers to meet Cornelius. Then he realised God was telling him that the gospel was for all people – Jews and Gentiles alike. A new chapter in the story of the Church was about to begin.

Interestingly, both Cornelius and Peter had their visions while they were offering their sacrifice of prayer. Things happen when people pray. People change and circumstances change. That is why Archbishop Donald Coggan wrote, 'Outside the room where a man is praying, the appropriate notice is not so much "Quiet! Man at prayer" as "Look out! God at work!" '[12]

Times for prayer
We can pray at any time, in any place. Some people even encourage us to be in prayer at *all* times and in *all* places. This was emphasised by the 17th-century monk Brother Lawrence, whose thoughts on the subject were recorded in a book entitled *The Practice of the Presence of God*. He taught that we can speak with God continually, acknowledge him in all we do and be constantly aware of his presence. He achieved this by what he called:

> ...a simple attention, and a general fond regard to God, which I may call an *actual presence of God*; or, to speak better, an habitual, silent, and secret conversation of the soul with God.[13]

Because he practised the presence of God, Brother Lawrence said he felt as close to God in the hectic, noisy monastery kitchen as he did in the tranquillity of the chapel.

Jesus was in constant communion with his heavenly Father but he also valued specific times of prayer (e.g. Mark 1:35; Matthew 14:23). If that was his experience, then how much more important it is for us to have regular, focused times of prayer. Many Christians find it good to begin their day in this way. Others prefer to set aside time during the day or at night. Some like to use all these times for prayer or to vary their prayer times.

These prayer times are sometimes referred to as a 'tryst'. This word, still common in Scotland, originates from the Old French word *tristre* which means 'waiting place'. It was once used in romantic novels to describe an agreement by two lovers to meet in a secret place at a certain time.

Jesus called his disciples to a tryst when he said, 'When you pray, go into your room, close the door and pray to your Father, who is unseen' (Matthew 6:6). He continued with a promise that this tryst would bring blessing: 'Then your Father, who sees what is done in secret, will reward you.'

Patterns for prayer
Various patterns for prayer have been devised to help us focus and make our prayer times more meaningful. One suggestion is to use a simple pattern based on the acrostic 'Acts' to remind us that prayer includes adoration, confession, thanksgiving and supplication (asking). [14]

Another model for prayer was outlined by Leslie Weatherhead who imagined prayer to be like seven rooms in a house in which we pray in different ways: [15]

Room 1	Affirm the presence of God
Room 2	Praise, thank and adore God
Room 3	Confession, forgiveness and unloading
Room 4	Affirmation and reception
Room 5	Purified desire and sincere petition
Room 6	Intercession for others
Room 7	Meditation

The 'house of prayer' pattern is used in the reflection at the end of chapter 13. This and other patterns remind us that there are different aspects of prayer. It is not just asking God to do something for us – prayer is much deeper and richer than that.

The sacrifice of prayer
Using a pattern for prayer is helpful, but the danger is that it can become a mere routine. When that happens, its purpose and power have been lost. Prayer is more than a routine – it is a relationship. In this sense

prayer is like sacrifice. Relationship is at the heart of prayer as it was at the heart of Old Testament sacrifices. Offerings were made as part of the people's covenant relationship with God. They could easily become empty rituals but the real purpose was to help the people keep their relationship with God alive and meaningful. The sacrifice of prayer has a similar purpose – it maintains and deepens our relationship with God. In prayer we get to know God better. We open our lives to him, share with him our deepest thoughts and feelings, seek his forgiveness and his grace, listen to his voice and submit ourselves to his will. In this way, prayer becomes an antidote to our self-centredness. The focus is on God. As Philip Yancey writes:

> In prayer I shift my point of view away from selfishness ...
> Prayer is the act of seeing reality from God's point of view. [16]

Prayer that develops our relationship with God comes from the heart, which means, like sacrifice, it can be costly. Watchman Nee makes this point when he describes how Old Testament sacrificial incense was produced from frankincense trees. He states:

> To obtain it, successive incisions were made in the bark, and the tree then oozed a white resin from which the incense was manufactured. Hence prayer is not the offering of just anything that might be at hand; it is the presenting of something drawn painfully out of the innermost heart, as though it seeped from our very wounds. [17]

Real prayer – sacrificial prayer – cannot just be about our superficial needs, desires or concerns. If our conversation with God is to be authentic we have to be completely open with him and speak with him about our deepest thoughts, feelings, motives and experiences. Some of these may lie hidden within our hearts and minds – buried deep down because they are too difficult to face. Being open with God means coming face to face with these things ourselves – and that can be an uncomfortable experience. It can also be painful to pour out our heartfelt concerns for others – family members, friends or even people we don't know personally but who are in desperate need. Such sacrificial prayer, drawn from the heart, is what deepens our relationship with God.

Prayer is also sacrificial because it means giving something up – time and effort. We may feel that time spent in prayer could be put to more practical use. There might be all sorts of tasks calling for our attention. Sacrificial prayer means letting go of the insistent desire to get on with things and spending time with God. Ole Hallesby highlights this sacrificial aspect of prayer:

> There is something about prayer and intercession which calls for more self-denial than any other work to which the Spirit calls us. [18]

He says this because of the time and effort that goes into secret prayer, which is 'neither seen nor appreciated'.

All this talk of sacrificial prayer might make us wonder whether it is worth the effort! But prayer is rewarding. Jesus said, 'Your Father, who sees what is done in secret, will reward you' (Matthew 6:6). By exploring different aspects of prayer in the next few chapters we will discover what these rewards are.

Chapter 11
Confessing

'CONFESSION is good for the soul.' Some people think this simply means that owning up to what they have done clears their conscience and makes them feel better about themselves. But true confession – confession to God – means more than that. It is a vital part of our spiritual experience. A Bible study leader once suggested that for every hour of prayer, five minutes should be spent in confession. Olive, one of the group members, had been a Christian since childhood. At first she was not convinced but she soon discovered the power of confession:

> This couldn't be meant for me. I didn't steal, swear, gamble or anything like that. Then God opened my eyes and I saw all the envy, hate and bitterness that had been stored up for years. For ten days I despaired of ever being right with God again. Then I allowed God to forgive me and at last I was back on speaking terms with him again. His life now flows through me, filling my whole being – I have a new relationship with him. [19]

An anatomy of sin

Psalm 32 helps us understand how confession renews and deepens our relationship with God. It begins by saying that a person is blessed when God forgives their sins:

> Blessed is the one
>   whose transgressions are forgiven,
>   whose sins are covered.
> Blessed is the one
>   whose sin the Lord does not count against them
>   and in whose spirit is no deceit.   (vv 1-2)

In these verses the psalmist uses three different Hebrew words to describe sin. The word translated as 'transgressions' means 'stepping over the line'. Sin sometimes involves doing what we should not do. These are known as sins of commission. The psalmist also refers to 'sin' using a word which means 'missing the target' or 'falling short of the standard'. We sin when we do not do what we should do. This happens when we fail to love God or our neighbour. These are sins of omission. Then the psalmist refers to 'deceit', a word meaning 'perverse' or 'twisted'. This is to do with inward motives rather than outward actions.

With this in mind it can be helpful to spend some moments in prayer at the end of the day reflecting on what has happened, asking the Holy Spirit to point out the things we should not have done, as well as the things we should have done but failed to do. The Spirit can also help us look deeper and identify thoughts, attitudes and motives that have been unworthy. All these things can be confessed before God.

What happens if sin is not confessed? In the next verses the psalmist shows how unconfessed and unforgiven sin had troubled him. It took a heavy toll, not just spiritually but physically and emotionally:

> When I kept silent,
>   my bones wasted away
>   through my groaning all day long.
> For day and night
>   your hand was heavy on me;
> my strength was sapped
>   as in the heat of summer.
>
> (vv 3–4)

Confession

Having thought about the effects of unconfessed sin, the psalmist decides to own up and seek forgiveness:

> Then I acknowledged my sin to you
>   and did not cover up my iniquity.
> I said, 'I will confess
>   my transgressions to the LORD.'
> And you forgave
>   the guilt of my sin.
>
> (v 5)

The psalmist realises he cannot cover up his sins. There can be no excuses, no explaining them away and no shifting the blame. They need to be acknowledged before God. He seems quite 'matter-of-fact' about this confession. But presumably there was more to it than simply telling God about his sins. God already knew all about them. What

God required was for the psalmist to sincerely acknowledge his sorrow for what he had done. Such sorrow is mentioned in another psalm where it is described as a sacrifice:

> You do not delight in sacrifice, or I would bring it;
>   you do not take pleasure in burnt offerings.
> My sacrifice, O God, is a broken spirit;
>   a broken and contrite heart
>   you, God, will not despise.
>
> (Psalm 51:16-17)

Experiencing sorrow for our sins is sacrificial. It costs us something to take a good look at ourselves and face up to what we have done. Understanding that we have fallen short of God's expectations and have spoilt our relationship with him can be a heartbreaking experience. More than that, becoming aware of our weakness is a blow to our pride and independence. In confession we sacrificially give up our self-sufficiency as we acknowledge our total dependence on God.

Although the expression of remorse is not mentioned in Psalm 32, presumably the psalmist did pour out his sorrow for his sins. Verse four indicates he was feeling the weight of conscience and it was this pent-up sense of guilt that must have formed part of his confession to God. None of us can truly confess our sins to God without regret. It is a sign of our sincerity – and we do need to be sincere in our confession if God is to forgive us.

Forgiveness

If we come before God in sincere confession, we can be sure he will forgive. It is in his nature to do so: 'If we confess our sins, he is faithful and just and will forgive us our sins and purify us from all unrighteousness' (1 John 1:9).

Going back to the opening verses of Psalm 32 we see what forgiveness involves. In verse one the word translated 'forgiven' means 'removed' or 'lifted'. When we are forgiven, the burden of guilt is lifted from us. The same verse speaks of sins being 'covered'. God chooses no longer to see our sins. Then verse two says the Lord does not 'count' our sins against us. Forgiveness is like having a debt cancelled.

A renewed relationship

Once his sins are forgiven the psalmist experiences a renewed relationship with God that gives him a deep sense of security:

> You are my hiding-place;
> > you will protect me from trouble
> > and surround me with songs of deliverance.   (v 7)

He also experiences the guidance of God:

> I will instruct you and teach you in the way you should go;
> > I will counsel you with my loving eye on you.   (v 8)

And he has the assurance of God's love and a sense of joy:

> Many are the woes of the wicked,
> > but the Lord's unfailing love
> > surrounds the one who trusts in him.
> Rejoice in the Lord and be glad, you righteous;
> > sing, all you who are upright in heart!   (vv 10-11)

The American pastor and writer Gordon MacDonald tells of a time when he and his wife decided to turn an overgrown field by their house into a meadow.[20] To do this they had to remove some rocks. They began with the largest, then the smaller ones and finally the smallest. It took more than two years – but that was not the end of it. They discovered that under the surface were many more rocks, some of them larger than the ones they had already cleared. These began to show above ground after each winter's frost and hit the blades of the mower as they cut the grass in the spring.

This process of turning the field into a meadow illustrates the need for ongoing confession. As we begin to examine our lives the obvious sins stand out. We confess them and receive forgiveness. Then smaller sins become visible and we deal with these also. But there are deeper, more dangerous sins – attitudes and motives – that only reveal themselves over time. Becoming aware of these and confessing them is part of the process of spiritual growth.

Sincere confession is good for the soul. It opens the way to a closer and deeper relationship with God. As such, it is a vital element of the sacrifice of prayer.

Chapter 12

Asking

THE English Baptist minister and social activist F. B. Meyer made a number of preaching trips to America at the end of the 19th and beginning of the 20th centuries. On one of his crossings he was asked to preach at the Sunday service and spoke about answered prayer.

A passenger who attended told his friends afterwards, 'I didn't believe a word of it.'

Later that day the passenger saw a woman on deck asleep in a chair with her hands lying open on her lap. He had two oranges in his pocket and, for a joke, placed one in each of her hands. When he came past later he saw her eating one of the oranges.

'You seem to be enjoying that,' he said.

'Yes,' she replied. 'I've been seasick for days and I was asking God somehow to send me an orange. I suppose I fell asleep while I was praying. When I woke up I found not one but two!'

The man went to hear Meyer preach again![21]

An unusual story, perhaps, but it illustrates an important aspect of prayer – asking. Jesus encouraged us to do it. He said:

> Ask and it will be given to you... If you, then, though you are evil, know how to give good gifts to your children, how much more will your Father in heaven give good gifts to those who ask him!
>
> (Matthew 7:7,11)

Jesus also taught his disciples to say, 'Give us today our daily bread' (Matthew 6:11).

Martin Luther comments that our daily bread is:

> ...everything that belongs to the support and wants of the body, such as meat, drink, clothing, shoes, house, homestead, field, cattle, money, goods, a pious spouse, pious children, pious servants, pious and faithful magistrates, good government,

good weather, peace, health, discipline, honour, good friends, faithful neighbours and the like. [22]

It seems that almost anything we need comes under the heading of daily bread! God cares about every detail of our lives and is willing to respond to our requests. We might wonder why we need to ask, if God is willing to give and knows our needs already. Perhaps it is because God wants us to be aware of our dependence on him. Even though we might work to earn money to provide for our needs, ultimately all we have comes from him. We are dependent on his provision. He asks us to ask him so that we do not take it all for granted. This sense of dependence is at the heart of our relationship with him.

In the name of Jesus
God does not give us everything we ask for, but the Bible helps us understand what kind of asking he will respond to. Jesus said:

> I will do whatever you ask in my name, so that the Father may be glorified in the Son. You may ask me for anything in my name, and I will do it.
> (John 14:13-14)

Jesus will answer requests made in his name, but this does not mean that simply using the name 'Jesus' in our prayers will guarantee an answer. It is not a magic word that makes all our wishes come true.

So what does it mean to pray in the name of Jesus? When we act in the name of someone, we are acting under their authority and with their approval. In the same way, to pray in the name of Jesus is to pray under his authority. It is to pray according to his will – to ask for something that meets with his approval. This takes great discernment, which comes with growing spiritual maturity – and even the greatest saints do not always get it right!

Doing something in the name of another person also means acting on their behalf. When we do this we act in ways that reflect their character because we do not want to misrepresent them or bring their name into disrepute. In a similar way, to pray in the name of Jesus is to pray for what is in line with his character. So, because Jesus is good, it means praying for things that are good and that will help to make us good.

For the glory of God

Jesus provided another clue to the way our requests are answered when he said the purpose of prayer is to bring glory to the Father – that is, to reveal God's goodness, greatness and grace.

Just as Old Testament sacrifices were sometimes wrongly seen as a way of manipulating God, so we can misuse our prayers to call on God to act according to our selfish purposes. James recognised this danger and pointed out that such prayers are not effective:

> When you ask, you do not receive, because you ask with wrong motives.
> (James 4:3)

We ask with wrong motives when we pray for anything that serves only our personal desires and ambitions. But we ask with right motives if our aim is always to glorify God.

When we pray to glorify God we are more likely to pray for qualities and characteristics than for material things. If our desire is to love God more deeply and to serve others more than we serve ourselves, then we should ask for wisdom to discern God's will, along with strength to do it, grace to reflect his love and opportunities to show it.

As Leslie Weatherhead wrote: 'We stop saying, "Give me," and start saying, "Make me" and "Show me" and "Use me".'[23] This kind of unselfish asking reminds us that we are called to live sacrificially for God – and prayer enables us to do so.

Asking for others

All that has been said about asking for ourselves applies to asking for others – intercession. But praying for others has an added dimension. When we intercede we are performing a priestly activity. Richard Foster explains why. He notes that Christians are called to be a holy priesthood, then writes:

> As priests, appointed and anointed by God, we have the honour of going before the Most High on behalf of others. This is not optional; it is a sacred obligation – and a precious privilege – of all who take up the yoke of Christ.[24]

Intercession is a responsibility to which God calls us all. And, as Dietrich Bonhoeffer notes, when it comes to praying for the people with whom we worship and serve, it is a vital responsibility: 'A Christian fellowship lives and exists by the intercession of its members for one another, or it collapses.' [25]

The motive for these prayers should always be love. In fact, without love it is almost impossible to pray for others as we should. It is easy to pray for the people we like – those who are dear to us or with whom we share common interests. It is not always easy to pray for those with whom we have differences or who mistreat us – even if they are fellow believers. But Jesus called us to 'love each other' (John 15:17) and to 'love your neighbour' (Mark 12:31). He even said, 'Love your enemies, do good to those who hate you' (Luke 6:27).

This kind of love is not a feeling. It is a determination to bless, to pray for and to seek the good of others, no matter who they are or what they have done. This is sacrificial prayer. It costs us something to pray like this. It is not natural, but by the grace of God we can do it – and he is glorified by it.

What is the answer?

If we do not pray in the name of Jesus and for the glory of God, the answer is likely to be 'no'. But even when we do pray in this way, the answer may not be a simple 'yes'. For example, if we pray for someone to become a Christian or to change in some way, our prayer may not be answered. God can influence them but will never force them against their will. They need to respond willingly to his promptings – his prevenient grace as it is called – and there is no guarantee that they will do so.

Sometimes God has other ways of answering our prayers – ways that will achieve his purposes more fully. We may not receive what we ask for immediately – in which case God's answer is, 'Be patient!' Or we may ask for something that we are already capable of doing, so his answer is, 'Do it yourself!' And sometimes he may be planning something better, so he says, 'Trust me!'

The call for patience and trust is even more necessary when situations appear to get worse after we have prayed! As Ann and Barry Ulanov point out: 'Prayers are sometimes answered by the experience of more struggle, by our being plunged into situations where we must risk more than we ever dared before.' [26]

Asking

Whatever the answer, God promises to be with us and to bless us. Perhaps this is what Jesus had in mind when he said, 'Your Father, who sees what is done in secret, will reward you' (Matthew 6:6). Answers to prayer are good, but the rewards of prayer are much richer and deeper. As Watchman Nee said, 'Prayer answered is secondary, while prayer rewarded is primary.'[27] Growing closer to God, learning to hear his voice, deepening our trust in him and growing in holiness – these are some of the rewards we are promised.

Ultimately prayer is a mystery, because God is infinitely wiser than we are. But we have the assurance that our prayers are heard and responded to in love. He knows what to give us better than we know what to ask for – and whatever his answers are, they will always be for our good.

> Praise be to God,
>   who has not rejected my prayer
>   or withheld his love from me!
> (Psalm 66:20)

Chapter 13
Listening

IT is easy to sympathise with Martha. Jesus and the disciples were in the house and while Martha was busy preparing a meal for them her sister Mary simply sat listening to Jesus. In the end it all got too much for her. 'Tell her to help me!' she said to Jesus. He responded, 'Martha, Martha, you are worried and upset about many things, but few things are needed – or indeed only one. Mary has chosen what is better, and it will not be taken away from her' (see Luke 10:38-42).

The Bible does not tell us what Martha said next! Perhaps she got the point and left the kitchen to join her sister at the feet of Jesus. Or perhaps not – because putting aside our activity to sit quietly and listen can be a difficult thing to do. It often seems so unproductive and unnecessary. Yet Jesus encouraged this because it is the 'better' thing to do.

Clearly Jesus was not saying that activity is unimportant. The story of Martha and Mary follows on from the parable of the good Samaritan, which concludes with Jesus' command: 'Go and do likewise' (Luke 10:37). We need to be actively involved in loving our neighbour but we also need to take time to meditate in prayer. Jesus was saying that there should be a balance. We are not to neglect one at the expense of the other. We must work for Jesus and listen to Jesus.

Meditation
The 19th-century Danish philosopher and theologian Søren Kierkegaard wrote:

> A man prayed, and at first he thought that prayer was talking. But he became more and more quiet until in the end he realised that prayer is listening.[28]

Other aspects of prayer allow us to speak or sing to God. In meditation we listen for his voice.

The idea of meditation is difficult for some Christians to accept. It sounds like something more suited to eastern religions like Buddhism. But meditation is a biblical practice. When Joshua became leader of the people of Israel, God said, 'Keep this Book of the Law always on your lips; meditate on it day and night' (Joshua 1:8). And the psalmist prayed, 'May these words of my mouth and this meditation of my heart be pleasing in your sight, LORD, my Rock and my Redeemer' (Psalm 19:14).

The aim of some forms of meditation is to empty the mind and become detached from the world in order to achieve inner harmony and peace. The aim of biblical meditation is to listen to God and be strengthened to obey, so that we can return to the world to make a difference for him. Inner peace is a wonderful side effect, but the main purpose is to help us grow in our relationship with God and to serve him better by serving others.

How do we listen to God in prayer? We can incorporate numerous forms of meditation into a daily prayer time. We may, for example, meditate on God's work in nature. But the most helpful form of meditation uses the Bible as its starting point. God has already spoken to us in the Bible and he speaks to us afresh as we meditate upon it.

Use your imagination
One kind of biblical meditation makes use of the imagination in connection with Gospel stories. Known as Ignatian contemplation, because it was encouraged by Ignatius of Loyola, the 16th-century founder of the Society of Jesus (Jesuits), it involves us imaginatively placing ourselves into an incident in the life of Jesus. We can use our senses as we do this. We see the sights, hear the sounds, even feel the objects in the story. We see Jesus at work and hear him speaking to us. We begin to imagine the thoughts, feelings and intentions of the people in the story – and our own thoughts, feelings and intentions as we become part of it. Through this imaginative meditation we discern what God wants to do for us. We also come to see what he wants us to do for him, and we dedicate ourselves to that task.

Take the story of Zacchaeus as an example (Luke 19:1-10). We can imagine ourselves in the crowd as Jesus approaches. We see the despised tax collector climb the sycamore tree and perhaps hear the crowd mocking him. Then Jesus calls his name. We see Zacchaeus climb down, feel the love that Jesus has for him and sense the astonishment of the crowd. We hear no words of condemnation from Jesus, but we witness Zacchaeus offering practical repentance and Jesus declaring that salvation has come to him. We realise that we, too, need to be open and honest with Jesus – and willing to put things right with other people. And as we see Jesus and Zacchaeus sharing a meal – a sign of true friendship in their culture – we realise that unconditional fellowship is also offered to us.

This kind of approach to the stories of Jesus seems to be encouraged by the way they were written. Although most English translations use the past tense, the original Greek is often in the present tense. The Gospel writers intended to make the stories vivid, drawing their readers into the action as if they were actually there when the incidents happened. The stories of Jesus are fertile ground for our God-given imagination. And using our imagination is a rewarding way to meditate.

Make a meal of it
A second kind of biblical meditation has an even longer history. It is the monastic practice emphasised in the sixth century by Benedict, and is known in Latin as *lectio divina* (sacred reading). Four steps are involved in this:

- Read
- Meditate
- Pray
- Contemplate.

They can be thought of as the stages of a meal.

First, we take a bite of food – we read the passage slowly and attentively several times. As we do so, a verse, a phrase, or even a single word, may stand out and become the focus of our attention.

Then we chew on it – we meditate on the word or phrase, turning it over in our mind, exploring how it makes us feel.

After that we savour its essence – we pray, talking with God about what the Spirit has revealed to us.

Finally, we digest it so that it nourishes us – in silence we allow the insight we have discovered to become part of us. We quieten our heart and mind and rest in God's love.

The idea of *lectio divina* is not to analyse verses to gain information as we might do in a Bible study – it is to allow the words to sink in and draw us closer to God. We should experience what the Bible is saying, not just understand it. So, for example, after reading the first chapter of John's Gospel a few times we might pause on verse 14, 'The Word became flesh and made his dwelling among us. We have seen his glory, the glory of the one and only Son, who came from the Father, full of grace and truth.'

We may be drawn to the phrase, 'full of grace' – and as we meditate on these words we might ask ourselves why they have caught our attention and what they mean for us in our present situation. Our thoughts might take us to other verses where grace is mentioned or where it is seen in practice.

We go where the Spirit leads and, as the full wonder of the phrase dawns on us, we become aware of how it makes us feel – thankful, excited, humble. Then we talk all this over with God, gratefully remembering times when we experienced grace or showed grace to others, telling him we are open to receive more and give more.

Finally, in silent contemplation, we are drawn deeper into God's presence to experience his peace and love.

The better way

Both types of meditation become more powerful as we practise them. As with anything we learn, it may seem as if we are making slow progress at first, but meditation is worth persisting with. It might be difficult – especially in the busyness of life – to sacrifice the time to listen carefully to God. But like Mary we should choose 'what is better' and not allow anything – or anyone – to take it from us. In sacrificing our time to listen we gain so much more than we lose.

Dietrich Bonhoeffer put it like this:

> Why do I meditate? Because I am a Christian and because therefore every day is a day lost for me in which I have not penetrated more deeply into the knowledge of the word of God in holy Scripture ... The word of Scripture should never stop sounding in your ears and working in you all the day long, just like the words of someone you love. [29]

—— *Reflection Three* ——

Praying

You are invited to use the 'house of prayer' pattern that was introduced in Chapter Ten. This model imagines prayer to be like the rooms of a house that are furnished with various Bible verses, thoughts and songs.

Room 1: Affirm the presence of God
Sit quietly for a moment, then use these words to help you become aware of the presence of God:

> Lord, I come before your throne of grace;
>   I find rest in your presence and fullness of joy.
> In worship and wonder I behold your face,
>   Singing, 'What a faithful God have I'.
>   (Robert and Dawn Critchley, *SASB* 378 v1) [30]

Room 2: Praise, thank and adore God
Write a list of the things to thank God for. Think about who he is and what he has done. Express your praise by reading Psalm 95:1-7.

Room 3: Confession, forgiveness and unloading
Be honest with God about your sins and failures. Tell him about your fears and worries.

> Cast all your anxiety on him because he cares for you.
>   (1 Peter 5:7)

Room 4: Affirmation and reception
Receive God's forgiveness, peace, power and love.

> When Jesus comes to you, he'll bring gladness,
> When Jesus comes to you, he'll bring peace.
> The glory of his presence from care will bring release,
>   When Jesus, Jesus comes to you.
>   (Joy Webb)

Room 5: Purified desire and sincere petition
Pray for yourself, remembering to ask in the name of Jesus and for the glory of God.

> Ask and it will be given to you;
> seek and you will find;
> knock and the door will be opened to you.
>
> (Matthew 7:7)

Room 6: Intercession for others
One way to pray for others is to begin with the people closest to you, then gradually widen the circle to include fellow Christians, friends, neighbours, colleagues and your community. There may also be national and international concerns that you can pray for.

> Some we love bear heavy burdens,
>   Some have wandered from the way;
> Be their guide, and their Deliverer,
>   Heavenly Father, now we pray.
> O'er our world so filled with sorrow,
>   Fear and hunger, pain and strife,
> Shed thy light of hope and mercy,
>   Gift of love, eternal life.
>
> (Doris Rendell, *SASB* 755 v2)

Room 7: Meditation
Read Mark 6:30-44.
Then close your eyes and enter into the story in your imagination.
As Jesus feeds the 5,000, let your senses take in what is happening.
Think about what the story means for you.
Let it lead you to worship, commitment and action.

Part Four

Praising

*Through Jesus, therefore,
let us continually offer to God a sacrifice of praise
– the fruit of lips that openly profess his name.
(Hebrews 13:15)*

Chapter 14
Let there be Praise!

HALLELUJAH! is one of the very few Hebrew words used around the world, whatever the native language. In everyday speech people often say 'hallelujah!' to express their relief that something they hoped for has happened. Someone might be on a station platform waiting for a train, which, after a long delay, finally arrives. Their frustrated wait is over so under their breath they mutter a 'hallelujah!' I doubt if the ancient Hebrews ever thought it would be used in this way! For them, it was not an expression of relief but an exclamation of joy and delight in God.

Praise the Lord!
'Hallelujah' is made up of two parts. The first part, 'hallelu', means 'praise'. The second part, 'jah' or 'yah', is a shortened form of YAHWEH, which is the Old Testament name for God. In English translations of the Bible YAHWEH is usually translated as 'the Lord', with the last three letters of 'Lord' in small capitals. So, when 'hallelujah' is translated into English it is 'praise the Lord'.

The Old Testament psalms again and again encourage us – even command us – to praise the Lord:

> Praise God in the great congregation;
> > praise the Lord in the assembly of Israel.   (68:26)
>
> Let everything that has breath praise the Lord.
> > Praise the Lord.   (150:6)

At other times the psalmist even tells his own soul to praise the Lord:

> Praise the Lord, my soul;
> > all my inmost being, praise his holy name.
>
> Praise the Lord, my soul,
> > and forget not all his benefits …   (103:1-2)

> Praise the LORD, my soul.
> LORD my God, you are very great;
> > you are clothed with splendour and majesty.   (104:1)

Why is there such an emphasis on praising God? The psalmist gives the answer, 'How good it is to sing praises to our God' (Psalm 147:1). We are expected to praise God because it is a good thing to do. Then the psalmist goes on to tell us why praise is good: '… how pleasant and how fitting to praise him'.

Pleasant praise
One of the reasons we praise another person for something they have done is to make them feel appreciated. But that is not a reason to praise God. He does not need to be congratulated in order to boost his self-esteem!

Praise is not for God's benefit, it is for ours. It opens our hearts to him and allows him to pour more of his grace and strength, more of his peace and joy, into our lives. When God calls us to praise him it is not really a demand, it is an offer – an offer to come close to him and receive more of him. As David Watson says, 'Whenever we honour God by giving him a sacrifice of praise, always he honours us.' [31]

God encourages us to praise him because it can help make us better people by releasing us from self-centredness. As Colin Gunton says:

> Praise… is the movement out of self into free and glad relationship with the other. To be truly human is, it must be realised, not to be curved in upon ourselves (one of Luther's definitions of sin) but to be liberated from self-preoccupation by and to the praise of God and each other. [32]

Not only does praise make us better people – it is actually one of the reasons for our existence. The first, and perhaps most famous, question of the Westminster Shorter Catechism is, 'What is the chief end of man?' ('end' means 'purpose'). The catechism answers, 'Man's chief end is to glorify God, and to enjoy him forever.'

The act of praising God is one way of glorifying and enjoying him – and in doing so we begin to find the real purpose of our lives. What could be more pleasant than that?

Fitting praise

The psalmist also says it is fitting to praise God. That means it is right and appropriate to praise God.

The Old Testament name for God, YAHWEH (which, as we saw earlier, is shown as 'the Lord' in many translations), is closely associated with the covenant that God made with his people. Moses discovered the meaning of this when he encountered God in the burning bush and received the call to lead his people out of Egypt:

> Moses said to God, 'Suppose I go to the Israelites and say to them, "The God of your fathers has sent me to you," and they ask me, "What is his name?" Then what shall I tell them?'
>
> God said to Moses, 'I AM WHO I AM. This is what you are to say to the Israelites: "I AM has sent me to you."'
>
> God also said to Moses, 'Say to the Israelites, "The Lord, the God of your fathers – the God of Abraham, the God of Isaac and the God of Jacob – has sent me to you."'
>
> (Exodus 3:13-15)

It was the Lord who would rescue them from Egypt. He would establish a covenant with them and continue to be faithful to them. The name 'the Lord' signified the covenant-making and covenant-keeping God – and this was something for which to praise him. He is still the God of the Covenant – faithful to his promises and committed to us in love, which was shown supremely in Jesus. So praise continues to be a fitting response and is part of what it means to be a living sacrifice.

Hebrews 13:15 says, '… let us continually offer to God a sacrifice of praise'. This comes near the end of the book, after the writer has detailed the way in which Jesus fulfilled the Old Testament sacrificial system by becoming the perfect high priest and sacrifice.

Jesus has opened the way for us to know God.

No wonder we are called to praise. Through him we can have a living relationship with the creator of the universe. We can know the covenant God who is almighty, loving and faithful. He is the one who guides, empowers and encourages us.

So, let there be praise! Hallelujah!

Chapter 15
Praise and Worship: Is there a Difference?

WHEN we express our devotion to God in singing we often distinguish between praise and worship. But is there a difference? If so, what is it?

Character and context

Some people think that praise and worship are distinguished by a different style or character of singing. Praise, they say, is noisy, joyful and up-tempo, whereas worship is quieter, slower, more devotional and more thoughtful. But this is not a valid distinction. If there is a difference, volume and tempo have very little to do with it.

Others say that praise and worship are distinguished by context. They understand praise to be a corporate activity as people join in praising God together. For example, Psalm 95:1 says, 'Come, let us sing for joy to the LORD; let us shout aloud to the Rock of our salvation'. Worship, on the other hand, is thought to be a more personal, intimate activity as we offer God our individual adoration, even if we are in a crowd. This does not seem wholly accurate either, because praise is sometimes a personal activity. So, in Psalm 103:1, the psalmist calls on 'my soul' and 'my inmost being' to praise God. You cannot get more personal than that!

The content of praise and worship

If there is a difference, perhaps it is in the content rather than the character or context of praise and worship. Leslie Weatherhead takes this approach. He says we praise and thank God for 'the way he has led us and for all he has done for us', but we adore him for 'all he is in himself', which means we 'call to mind his attributes and remember his love, his splendour, his power, his beauty, his wisdom, his holiness'. [33] So the idea is that praise is given for what God does and worship is given for who he is.

When we look at the Bible, however, praise and worship do not fall so neatly into these two categories. For example, Psalm 100:4-5 gives God praise for his attributes – his goodness, love and faithfulness – rather than what he does:

> Enter his gates with thanksgiving
>   and his courts with praise;
>   give thanks to him and praise his name.
> For the LORD is good and his love endures for ever;
>   his faithfulness continues through all generations.

Another approach is to say that when we praise we sing *about* God – we sing to others and to ourselves about his greatness, his goodness and his faithfulness. But when we worship we sing *to* God – we express our adoration, our thanks and our trust directly to him. If this is the difference, though, it does not seem a very great one.

What is worship?
Perhaps we should think more carefully about what we mean by worship. So far we have thought of worship as something we do – singing songs or offering prayers. But worship is primarily an attitude of submission and humility. In the Bible this attitude is expressed outwardly in kneeling, bowing or lying prostrate on the ground as, for example, in Psalm 95:6,

> Come, let us bow down in worship, let us kneel before the LORD
> our Maker.

And Revelation 4:10 tells us:

> … the twenty-four elders fall down before him who sits on the
> throne and worship him who lives for ever and ever.

The attitude of submission can be expressed in words. These words can be spoken or sung, as we see in the many prayers of the psalms – prayers of confession, prayers of trust and prayers of obedience.

And Philippians 2:10-11 points to a time when 'at the name of Jesus' not only should 'every knee' bow, but there will also be a spoken expression of submission:

> … and every tongue acknowledge that Jesus Christ is Lord, to
> the glory of God the Father.

Worship, too, was expressed in the sacrificial system as outlined in the Old Testament. When a sacrifice was made the worshippers were giving themselves to God. It was an outward expression of their covenant relationship with him and their obedience to him. Part of the ritual of sacrifice included praise and thanksgiving. Psalm 27:6 states:

> At his sacred tent I will sacrifice with shouts of joy;
> I will sing and make music to the LORD.

There were even musical priests with responsibility for leading praise (2 Chronicles 7:6; 8:14).

Being a 'living sacrifice', as the New Testament calls us to be, is also an outward expression of worship. We submit ourselves totally to God and so worship him with every aspect of our lives – our relationships, our work, the way we speak and the way we act. By doing this we are also praising him. Lives lived and words spoken for God reflect his goodness and faithfulness – they are an offering of praise to him.

Worship as an attitude of submission to God is described beautifully in the memorable words of William Temple:

> Worship is the submission of all our nature to God. It is the quickening of conscience by his holiness; the nourishment of the mind with his truth; the purifying of the imagination by his beauty; the opening of the heart to his love; the surrender of the will to his purpose – and all this gathered up in adoration, the most selfless emotion of which our nature is capable. [34]

This description of adoration as 'the most selfless emotion of which our nature is capable' is similar to Colin Gunton's comment about praise in Chapter 14. He described praise as 'the movement out of self into free and glad relationship with the other'. [35] Thus worship and praise are similar in that they both turn our attention away from ourselves and towards God.

One great stream of response
It seems from all this that there is no clear distinction between praise and worship. We may try to distinguish them in theory, but in reality the lines are blurred – the two can overlap. Worship is primarily an

attitude of submission to God, which is seen in our actions and our words. Some of these words are words of praise – and when they are sung they are songs of praise! So, worship leads to praise.

But it is also true that praise leads to worship. As we praise God, reminding ourselves of all that he is and does and has done, we are led to submit our lives more deeply.

Perhaps the best way to understand it is to think of praise and worship as partners together in our response to God. In praise we acknowledge God's goodness, his greatness and his faithfulness. As we do this we also express our love for him, our confidence in him and our submission to him – and that is worship. Each helps the other to be more meaningful – and each complements the other as we respond to the grace of God with our lips and with our lives. Selwyn Hughes writes that although there is a distinction between worship, praise and thanksgiving, 'it must not be regarded as hard and fast. They flow into each other to form one great stream'.[36] When we think of it this way, perhaps praise and worship are not so different after all!

Chapter 16
Let All Things their Creator Bless!

IN the centre of Barcelona stands the Basilica of La Sagrada Família (The Holy Family). Designed by the Spanish Catalan architect Antoni Gaudí, it is one of the most amazing and controversial churches in the world. Building work began in 1882 and is not likely to finish until 2026, which is the centenary of Gaudí's death. Even so, it has been declared a Unesco World Heritage Site.

Gaudí's design was inspired by the natural world. He used geometric forms based on nature throughout the building, which is full of twists, spirals and curved surfaces. The tops of some of the spires look like the lavender, wheat and grasses that grow in the Catalan region, while others resemble piles of apples and oranges or clusters of grapes.

Some of the most striking features inside the church are the central columns, which rise to different heights and are constructed to look like the trees of a forest. They support a vaulted ceiling resembling branches and leaves spreading out like the canopy of a forest. The soft light filtering through the stained-glass windows adds to the effect.

Some might think that all this is in praise of nature. But actually, it represents nature's praise of God. It is as if creation is there, alongside God's people, offering its own praises.

Creation's praises
The wonderful poetry of the psalms describes the whole of creation singing in joyful praise:

> Let the heavens rejoice, let the earth be glad;
>   let the sea resound, and all that is in it.
> Let the fields be jubilant, and everything in them;
>   let all the trees of the forest sing for joy.
> Let all creation rejoice before the LORD ...
>   (Psalm 96:11-13)

> Let the sea resound, and everything in it,
>> the world, and all who live in it.
> Let the rivers clap their hands,
>> let the mountains sing together for joy;
>> let them sing before the LORD ...
>
> (Psalm 98:7-9)

St Francis of Assisi took his cue from the psalmist when he wrote a hymn of praise which pictures nature joining in with the praises of God's people.

It is worth quoting in full:

> All creatures of our God and King,
> Lift up your voice and with us sing
>> Alleluia, alleluia!
> Thou burning sun with golden beam,
> Thou silver moon with softer gleam:
>
> *O praise him, O praise him,*
> *Alleluia, alleluia, alleluia!*
>
> Thou rushing wind that art so strong,
> Ye clouds that sail in heaven along,
>> O praise him, alleluia!
> Thou rising morn, in praise rejoice,
> Ye lights of evening, find a voice:
>
> Thou flowing water, pure and clear,
> Make music for thy Lord to hear,
>> Alleluia, alleluia!
> Thou fire so masterful and bright,
> That givest man both warmth and light:
>
> Dear mother Earth, who day by day
> Unfoldest blessings on our way,
>> O praise him, alleluia!
> The flowers and fruits that in thee grow,
> Let them his glory also show:

> Let all things their Creator bless,
> And worship him in humbleness,
>   O praise him, alleluia!
> Praise, praise the Father, praise the Son,
> And praise the Spirit, Three in One:
>
> *O praise him, O praise him,*
> *Alleluia, alleluia, alleluia!*
>
> (SASB 2)

Of course, all this is poetic imagination but it does express a truth – creation praises God. The mountains cannot sing and the rivers do not have hands to clap, nevertheless creation praises God by its very existence.

In the same way that we praise God by living for him and fulfilling his purposes for us, so creation praises him by being and doing what he created it to be and do. It reflects the glory of God – the Creator, Preserver and Governor of all things – simply by being. Psalm 19 says as much:

> The heavens declare the glory of God;
>   the skies proclaim the work of his hands.
> Day after day they pour forth speech;
>   night after night they reveal knowledge.
> They have no speech, they use no words;
>   no sound is heard from them.
> Yet their voice goes out into all the earth,
>   their words to the ends of the world.
>
> (Psalm 19:1-4)

So, creation praises God by silently going about its work. Sometimes, of course, it is not silent. Creation can make a joyful noise to the Lord! When the ocean waves boom, when the wind whistles in the trees, when the lions roar and the birds sing, they are praising God by doing what they were made to do. And they are producing sounds – sounds that we can think of as their songs of praise.

If nature praises God by being what he created it to be, human beings should not stand in the way of creation's praise. Too often people have abused or destroyed God's good creation. To do this is not only to disobey God's command to 'work it and take care of it' (Genesis 2:15), it is also to deny nature its opportunity to praise God. In a sense, when we devastate tropical rain forests, pollute rivers and endanger species, we are withdrawing praise from God by not allowing nature to fulfil its purpose.

Instead, we should 'let all things their Creator bless!'

Voicing creation's praises
But even when nature is doing what nature does – whether silently or noisily – it is not doing it intentionally. Creation does not make a conscious effort to praise God. That is what human beings do. And because nature cannot consciously do it, when we praise God, we also do it on behalf of all creation.

David Hart calls human beings 'the priesthood of creation that unites Earth to Heaven'.[37] As Old Testament priests offered sacrifices to God on behalf of the people of God, so we, as 'a holy priesthood, offering spiritual sacrifices' (1 Peter 2:5), offer praise to God on behalf of nature. It is our priestly privilege to voice the praises of creation as we offer a sacrifice of praise.

> Good Lord God, creator of the universe, watch over us and keep us in the light of your presence. May our praise continually blend with that of all creation, until we come together to the eternal joys which you promise in your love. Amen.
> (John Henry Jowett)

Chapter 17
A Costly Sacrifice

ON his BBC Radio 5 Live film review show, presenter Simon Mayo once asked the listeners to name films that included no negative thoughts, feelings or experiences. Many suggestions were emailed and texted in, but the show's film critic, Mark Kermode, was able to identify some element of negativity in every one of them. It was impossible to find a film of any reasonable quality that was completely positive. Even the best 'feel good' films had some sadness, tension or darkness in them. Kermode and Mayo concluded that any good film includes both positive and negative – and any film that does not have them is not very good! The reason for this is obvious. Films reflect life – and life is not always positive. It is a mixture of joy and sorrow, hope and despair, the good, the bad and the ugly.

Rejoice in the Lord always!
The Bible asks us to '... continually offer to God a sacrifice of praise' (Hebrews 13:15). To offer praise continually means to do it in all circumstances – when we are down as well as when we are up, in the darkness as well as in the light, through the rough times as well as the smooth.

Paul says something similar to the church at Philippi, 'Rejoice in the Lord always. I will say it again: rejoice!' (Philippians 4:4). The Philippians knew Paul meant it, because it was during tough times in Philippi that he had done just that. Paul and Silas were attacked by a crowd and arrested by the magistrates – then stripped, beaten, flogged and thrown into prison. Despite this, they offered God their sacrifice of praise:

> About midnight Paul and Silas were praying and singing hymns to God, and the other prisoners were listening to them.
> (Acts 16:25)

This cannot have been easy. They were bruised and shaken, and perhaps feeling unjustly treated, yet they continued to praise.

Praising God may be easy when life is good and all is well. But when things are not so good praising can be the last thing we feel like doing. It is then that praise becomes a costly sacrifice. How do we praise God when our circumstances give us no reason to do so? It is likely that Paul and Silas were singing hymns they had memorised from the Old Testament hymn book – the Book of Psalms. That is where we find some clues about how to offer a sacrifice of praise.

Praise and lament
The psalms reflect a wide variety of human moods and circumstances. John Calvin called the psalms 'an anatomy of all the parts of the soul' because 'there is not an emotion of which any one can be conscious that is not here represented as in a mirror'.[38] This full range of human emotions is expressed in the two main types of psalm: hymns of praise and psalms of lament.[39] The shortest psalm, Psalm 117, is an example of a hymn of praise. It begins with a call to praise, continues with reasons for praise by describing the character of God and concludes with a further call to praise:

> Praise the LORD, all you nations;
>   extol him, all you peoples.
> For great is his love towards us,
>   and the faithfulness of the LORD endures for ever.
> Praise the LORD.

The second type – psalms of lament – can include a complaint to God about the psalmist's situation, a prayer for help and an affirmation of trust in God. They can also contain a confession of sin or a plea of innocence, a prayer for forgiveness and even a call for vengeance. They usually conclude with a vow to praise God.

Psalm 13 is an example:

> How long, LORD? Will you forget me for ever?
> How long will you hide your face from me?
> How long must I wrestle with my thoughts
>   and day after day have sorrow in my heart?
> How long will my enemy triumph over me?

> Look on me and answer, LORD my God.
> Give light to my eyes, or I will sleep in death,
>   and my enemy will say, 'I have overcome him,'
>   and my foes will rejoice when I fall.
> But I trust in your unfailing love;
>   my heart rejoices in your salvation.
> I will sing the LORD's praise,
>   for he has been good to me.

Worship needs to include both praise and lament. If our worship is all 'happy clappy' it is not true to life. Praise loses meaning, depth and vitality if it leaves no room for lament that acknowledges difficulties – the pain, struggle, disappointment and doubt that are so often part of life. Lament does not have the final word though. Even in psalms of lament the movement is towards praise. We see this in Psalm 13 where the psalmist pleads for God to answer and help him in his distress but ends with a determination to sing praise to God.

Such praise can be a costly sacrifice. Watchman Nee writes:

> In its nature praise is sacrifice. Not only must we exalt his name when we stand on the summit and view the promised land; we must learn also to compose psalms of confidence in him when we walk through the valley of the shadow of death. This is praise in truth. [40]

In sorrow there can be a sacrifice of praise – a costly sacrifice because it is offered from the depths of despair.

Faith is the key

How is this costly sacrifice possible? When we look carefully at the psalms of lament we often see a statement that marks a turning point. In Psalm 13 it comes in verse 5, 'But I trust in your unfailing love'. No explanation is given for this change of mood. The most likely reason is that the psalmist has committed the matter to God and realises that, whatever happens and however he feels, God is with him, holding him securely. He knows God's love will never fail. His circumstances have not changed but he sees beyond them to the faithfulness of God. He may not feel like shouting and dancing for joy but he has a deep confidence in God that allows his heart to rejoice and 'sing the LORD's praise'.

Hebrews 13:15 says our sacrifice of praise is 'the fruit of lips that openly profess his name'. Professing his name means acknowledging his goodness and trusting in his love for us. It is from this trust that our praises come in the bad times as well as the good. The key to offering a continual sacrifice of praise is faith in the God of love, even when we do not feel the love of God.

The sacrifice of praise is not an effort to cheer ourselves up when times are tough – it is the fruit of our confidence in God. It was this kind of confidence that allowed Paul and Silas to sing to God in prison in Philippi – a confidence summed up by Paul when he writes:

> And we know that in all things God works for the good of those who love him, who have been called according to his purpose.
> (Romans 8:28)

In the ups and downs of life, we can continually offer up a sacrifice of praise.

—— Reflection Four ——
Praising

For this reflection you are invited to engage with Scripture, prayerfully using the ancient spiritual discipline of *lectio divina* which was outlined in Chapter 13. A verse or passage is chosen and read slowly and prayerfully, taking time to meditate on particular words or phrases as you feel led. There is no pressure to 'finish' the reading if you feel drawn to stay with a single word or phrase.

- Read
- Meditate
- Pray
- Contemplate.

The pattern is to read and meditate, listening to what God is saying through his word. This leads into prayer as you respond to him. Express what you have discovered, offering your thoughts and feelings, knowing that you are loved and accepted by God.

Then contemplate – continuing to reflect on the Scripture as if it is a precious jewel you want to see from every angle. You may repeat the pattern several times, moving through a verse or passage, but there are no set rules.

Your time of *lectio divina* might result in a particular commitment or action, but the primary aim is simply to be in the presence of God.

As a starting point take yourself to a place where you can be silent and still. Ask God to guide you, teach you and speak to you as you meditate on one of the following verses:

> Through Jesus, therefore, let us continually offer to God a sacrifice of praise – the fruit of lips that openly profess his name.
>
> (Hebrews 13:15)

> May these words of my mouth and this
> meditation of my heart
> be pleasing in your sight,
> Lord, my Rock and my Redeemer.
>
> (Psalm 19:14)

A life of praise in every part

It may be that, following chapters on the theme of praise, you were expecting a reflection that encouraged a lively response.

Here are a few ideas:

- *Take a walk with the Lord in a beautiful natural location, praising God for what you see, hear and feel.*

- *Take a walk in your neighbourhood or near your workplace, praising God for what you see, hear and feel.*

- *Put some music on and sing.*
  Put some music on and dance!
  Let this be an offering of praise to the Lord.

Part Five

Serving

*... I am being poured out like
a drink offering on the sacrifice
and service coming from your faith ...
(Philippians 2:17)*

Chapter 18
In the Ministry

THE Reformation in the 16th century turned the Church upside down. Beliefs and practices that had developed over previous centuries were challenged by reformers such as Martin Luther and John Calvin in an attempt to recover biblical Christianity. One of the principles that emerged was that of the priesthood of all believers, which stated that all Christians have direct access to God, by grace, through faith, so that we do not need an earthly priest to mediate for us. This was a wonderfully liberating rediscovery of a profound biblical truth. The complementary truth is that all Christians are able to serve God – which is perhaps more helpfully described as the ministry of all believers.

Many churches reserve the title 'minister' for a full-time ordained leader – someone who is 'in the ministry'. The danger is that others can fail to play their part, leaving all the ministry to the minister. A church member once complained to his minister that someone had come to him needing help. He had rung the church office, but no one was there. The church member had to help the person himself. He told the minister that it was a shame the church could not do anything. 'It looks as if the church did!' the minister replied.

The full-time ordained minister's role is 'to focus the mission and ministry of the whole Church so that its members are held faithful to their calling'.[41] And the calling that every Christian is to be held faithful to is to be a minister.

'Minister' is a Latin word meaning 'servant' – and 'to minister' means 'to serve' or 'to wait upon'. Although it indicates a menial role, in the Old Testament 'servant of God' was a title of honour. It was used of Moses (Exodus 14:31) and David (2 Samuel 3:18).

In the New Testament Paul often described himself as a 'servant of God' or a 'servant of Jesus Christ'. He also called his fellow believers 'servants'. Paul wrote to the Philippians referring to 'the sacrifice and service coming from your faith' (Philippians 2:17). Their work for God and for one another – their ministry – was a sacrificial service.

Jesus, the servant
The greatest expression of sacrificial service was Jesus, who 'did not come to be served, but to serve, and to give his life as a ransom for many' (Mark 10:45). When Jesus spoke of himself as a servant he would have had in mind the Servant Songs of Isaiah (42:1-4; 49:1-6; 50:4-9; 52:13 to 53:12). These verses depict God's anointed and obedient Servant who would bring justice and salvation through the voluntary giving of his life for the sins of the people. This was how Jesus saw himself. He lived and died in the service of God, for the sake of others.

The disciples witnessed this in a dramatic and memorable way at the Last Supper. When guests arrived for a meal, having walked the dusty roads in sandals, they would normally find water pots by the door and a servant to wash their feet.

But at the Last Supper there was no servant to do this. Jesus got up, took off his robe, wrapped a towel round his waist, filled a bowl with water and began to wash and dry the disciples' feet. This must have astonished them. Here was their Master humiliating himself. Peter was the one who voiced their thoughts: 'Lord, are you going to wash my feet?' (John 13:6).

By this simple act Jesus gave the disciples an example of loving, sacrificial service:

> Now that I, your Lord and Teacher, have washed your feet, you also should wash one another's feet. I have set you an example that you should do as I have done for you.
> (John 13:14-15)

But the act of washing the disciples' feet was more than an example of service for them to follow. It had a much deeper meaning. It was a picture of Jesus' whole life of service – service that brought him from Heaven and took him to the Cross.

This becomes clear when we put the actions of Jesus at the Last Supper alongside the words of one of the earliest hymns of the Church, which Paul outlines in Philippians 2:6-11.

John 13	Philippians 2

Jesus was the Son of God —

'Jesus knew that the Father had put all things under his power, and that he had come from God and was returning to God;	'...being in very nature God, [he] did not consider equality with God something to be* used to his own advantage;
(v 3)	(v 6)

but he became a servant —

so he got up from the meal, took off his outer clothing, and wrapped a towel round his waist.	rather, he made himself nothing by taking the very nature of a servant, being made in human likeness.
(v 4)	(v 7)

to cleanse us from our sins by his death for us —

After that he poured water into a basin and began to wash his disciples' feet...	And being found in appearance as a man, he humbled himself by becoming obedient to death – even death on a cross!
(v 5)	(v 8)

then returned to his rightful place in Glory

...When he had finished washing their feet, he put on his clothes and returned to his place.'	Therefore God exalted him to the highest place and gave him the name that is above every name, that at the name of Jesus every knee should bow, in heaven and on earth and under the earth, and every tongue acknowledge that Jesus Christ is Lord, to the glory of God the Father.'
(v 12)	(vv 9-11)

---

* Many editions of the *New International Version* simply say 'grasped' at this point (Ed).

The mundane act of foot washing symbolised the momentous act of redemption. Both were expressions of the servant heart of Jesus and both were examples for his followers. They were to emulate him in their actions – 'do as I have done for you' (John 13:15) and in their attitudes – 'have the same mindset as Christ Jesus' (Philippians 2:5).

The servant Church

On Easter Sunday evening the disciples were once again gathered together in a room. So much had happened since the Last Supper three nights before. Jesus had been arrested, tried and crucified. Now there were reports that he had risen from the dead. They must have been confused and afraid. But Jesus appeared to them and said, 'Peace be with you!' (John 20:19) then added, 'As the Father has sent me, I am sending you' (v 21). In these words, he summed up their calling to be servants of God and servants of all. The calling and sending of Jesus by the Father was the basis of the calling and sending of the disciples by Jesus. His servant-response to the Father was the foundation and motivation of their servant-response to him.

The same has been true for every follower of Jesus since then. Ours is not a new and different mission. It is simply the extension of the work that Jesus began.

His physical presence is absent, but the Church is his body – his hands, his feet, his mouth – serving God and serving the world. He is the pattern for our actions and our attitudes. More than that – it is he, by his Spirit, who continues to work through the life and ministry of the Church.

The servant Church does the servant work of Jesus with the servant heart of Jesus. Every individual is called into the ministry of Jesus, giving themselves in 'sacrifice and service' (Philippians 2:17).

Chapter 19
The Roots of Service

IN the previous chapter, we saw that, when Jesus washed his disciples' feet at the Last Supper, he not only offered them a simple act of service, he was also symbolising his entire ministry – from the cradle to the Cross, and beyond. Before the action begins, though, there is a verse that takes us deep into his heart and mind, showing what prompted his act of service:

> Jesus knew that the Father had put all things under his power, and that he had come from God and was returning to God.
> (John 13:3)

Three aspects of the way Jesus understood and experienced his relationship with the Father are made clear in this verse. They help us see how being rooted in God can nurture sacrificial service.

'Jesus knew that the Father had put all things under his power'
Jesus was empowered by the Father. It was this that enabled him to heal, teach, cast out demons and raise the dead. Amazing power was at his disposal and his understanding of where it had come from enabled him to use it to serve others instead of himself.

It was God's power, and because God is love, Jesus used that power in love. Love 'is not self-seeking' (1 Corinthians 13:5) so Jesus used his power in love to serve others. The first temptation Jesus experienced in the desert at the beginning of his ministry was to use this power for himself instead of for others. He had fasted for 40 days and nights and must have been extremely hungry. The Devil then tempted him to turn stones into bread. But Jesus knew the purpose of his power was not to satisfy his own physical hunger – it was to serve others by satisfying their spiritual hunger. So he responded:

> It is written: 'Man shall not live on bread alone, but on every word that comes from the mouth of God.'
> (Matthew 4:4)

The power of the Holy Spirit is available to every Christian to enable us to do God's work. The temptation we face is to enjoy the Spirit's presence, with all the blessings he brings, but not to use his power to serve others. Like Jesus, we need to resist that temptation and channel this spiritual power into loving service – because the Father who has given it to us is love.

This insight into the mind of Jesus also has something to say about the use of authority. If we are given any authority – in the Church, in our working lives or in any other sphere – we are to use it in love. Jesus saw how authority could be abused and he called his disciples to a better way. He said:

> You know that the rulers of the Gentiles lord it over them, and their high officials exercise authority over them. Not so with you. Instead, whoever wants to become great among you must be your servant, and whoever wants to be first must be your slave – just as the Son of Man did not come to be served, but to serve, and to give his life as a ransom for many.
> (Matthew 20:25-28)

At The Salvation Army's William Booth College in London there is a stone plaque in the ground by one of the footpaths. It simply says, 'By love, serve.' That sums up what was going through the mind of Jesus at the Last Supper and describes the way his followers must act.

'Jesus knew ... that he had come from God'

Jesus was well aware of his own identity. He knew where he was from and who he was. He was from God and he was the Son of God.

Mark 14:36 records a prayer of Jesus in which he uses the word *Abba* to address God. It is one of the few New Testament words recorded in Aramaic – the language that Jesus spoke – and it means 'father'. It was a word used in intimate family relationships but was never applied to God. For Jesus, however, it expressed the deep and intimate relationship that he had with the Father.

It was from the strength of this relationship that Jesus could serve. Knowing who he was enabled him to stoop to wash the disciples' feet. His awareness of his true identity as the Son of God allowed him to reach out in humility as the servant of God and the servant of all.

We are children of God. He loves us, has saved us and has brought us into his family. This is our primary identity – and it is on this basis that we serve others. Understanding who we are gives us the sense of security, self-worth and significance that we need to be servants. If we look for our sense of worth in what we do, then when we are called to serve and to do what seems insignificant or demeaning, we could feel worthless and insignificant. We may well resist the call to service, preferring instead to preserve our dignity and hold on to our self-esteem. But, when we find our sense of worth in our identity as eternally loved children of God, we can be humble servants.

'Jesus knew ... that he ... was returning to God'
At the Last Supper Jesus knew he was about to be crucified. This knowledge must have dominated his thoughts and emotions, yet he was able to see beyond the Cross to the time when he would return to his Father. This was 'the joy that was set before him' (Hebrews 12:2) that enabled him to endure suffering and death. Jesus saw beyond the horizon of immediate circumstances to the eventual outcome. He was aware of the journey he had to make but he was also sure of the destination. It was not only this personal hope that inspired Jesus. There was also the knowledge that he was serving his Father's saving purpose. To create a new humanity and renew creation he became the servant of all and was obedient to death. To shape the Church that was to come he gave an example of servanthood characterised by humility, love and sacrifice.

Like Jesus, we need a vision of the future that inspires us to serve and enables us to sacrifice. Peter says, 'we are looking forward to a new heaven and a new earth, where righteousness dwells' (2 Peter 3:13). This is the vision of the future that inspires us for today. It helps us work for the Kingdom of God to become a reality in the lives of those whom we serve, in the hope that one day every knee will bow and every tongue acknowledge that Jesus Christ is Lord.

The greatest example
The servant attitude and servant ministry of Jesus were rooted in his intimate relationship with God the Father. In this he set us the greatest example. Richard Foster says, 'True service comes from a relationship with the divine Other deep inside.' [42] In our relationship with God we, like Jesus, find the source of our servant attitude and servant ministry.

Chapter 20
Full Equipment for the Task

WHEN Jesus said to the disciples, 'As the Father has sent me, I am sending you' (John 20:21), they probably wondered how they could possibly fulfil this calling. If they were concerned about this, they would have been relieved by his next words, 'Receive the Holy Spirit' (v 22).

Jesus was pointing forward to Pentecost, when the Spirit would be poured out on them. It was a reminder that, although they were called to a daunting task, they were to have the powerful presence of the Spirit with them. The Spirit would enable them to be effective servants of their Servant Lord. Just as the call to serve in the footsteps of Jesus was not limited to the disciples who first heard it but extends to us all, so the promise of the Spirit is for us all.

In the words of John Gowans:

> Still God gives his willing servant
> Full equipment for the task;
> Power is found by those who seek it,
> Grace is given to those who ask.
>
> (*SASB* 34 v 4)

Gifts of the Spirit
The Spirit is given to every Christian. After all, it is by the Spirit that we are born again as children of God. There is no such thing as a Spiritless Christian. With the gift of the Spirit come the gifts of the Spirit. If the gift of the Spirit makes us children of God, the gifts of the Spirit equip us to be servants of God and servants of one another. These gifts are, as John Stott says, 'certain capacities, bestowed by God's grace and power, which fit people for specific and corresponding service'.[43]

The New Testament lists a variety of gifts:

- Romans 12:6-8 – prophesying, serving, teaching, encouraging, giving, leading, showing mercy.
- 1 Corinthians 12:8-10 – a message of wisdom, a message of knowledge, faith, healing, miraculous powers, prophecy,

distinguishing between spirits, speaking in different kinds of tongues, the interpretation of tongues.
- 1 Corinthians 12:28 – apostles, prophets, teachers, miracles, healing, helping, guidance, different kinds of tongues.
- Ephesians 4:11 – apostles, prophets, evangelists, pastors, teachers.
- 1 Peter 4:9-11 – hospitality, speaking, serving.

These lists include a varied mixture of gifts. Some are miraculous, others quite ordinary. Some are public, others are private. Some make a spiritual and pastoral impact, others a physical impact. Some are for use within the Church, others are to benefit those outside the Church.

It is important to understand that the gifts mentioned in the New Testament are not the only ones that God gives. And often it is our natural abilities – which after all, are God-given – that he turns into spiritual gifts. Some of those mentioned in the New Testament are like this – for example serving, encouraging and hospitality.

But we can also think of artistic talents (e.g. writing, drawing, singing or playing a musical instrument); practical abilities (e.g. designing and making things); or relational skills (e.g. listening and counselling). When natural talents such as these are dedicated to God's service they can be enhanced and used by the Spirit – and they become spiritual gifts.

Albert Orsborn, General of The Salvation Army from 1946 to 1954, revealed how his poetic talent was dedicated to God as a spiritual gift:

> I wanted to go to a better school, a college, a university; to give my nature wings, to study poetry for the sheer love of it, for my own self-expression and satisfaction. Instead, my Saviour called me to bring my love of poetry and song and nail it with my own willing hands to his Cross, if maybe some word of mine might be used in his service.[44]

How the Spirit works with our natural abilities to produce spiritual gifts is something of a mystery. But Samuel Shoemaker helps us understand it a little better:

> Something comes into our energies and capacities and expands them. We are laid hold of by something greater than ourselves. We can face things, create things, accomplish things, that in our

own strength would have been impossible ... The Holy Spirit seems to mix and mingle his power with our own, so that what happens is both a heightening of our own powers, and a gift to us from outside. [45]

Common characteristics

Although there is a great variety of gifts, they all have important features in common. To begin with, they all come from the same source. They are gifts from God to be received gratefully and used faithfully. Paul writes:

> There are different kinds of gifts, but the same Spirit distributes them. There are different kinds of service, but the same Lord. There are different kinds of working, but in all of them and in everyone it is the same God at work.
> (1 Corinthians 12:4-6)

Secondly, spiritual gifts are all chosen for us. They are given by God 'just as he determines' (1 Corinthians 12:11). We do not get to choose which gifts we receive, or how many. They are not rewards for our goodness, intelligence or achievements. They are gifts of grace – given freely and undeservedly. God knows which gifts suit us best, and what part we can play most effectively in the life of his Church and his mission. It is true that Paul wrote, 'Eagerly desire the greater gifts' (1 Corinthians 12:31), but that is not to say we will receive them! As with all answers to prayer, God will ensure that we receive what is best, according to his good and perfect will. What we can be sure of is that we all have at least one gift and that we have a responsibility to use it.

Thirdly, spiritual gifts are all for the service of others. Paul tells us that 'the manifestation of the Spirit is given for the common good' (1 Corinthians 12:7) and Peter says, 'Each of you should use whatever gift you have received to serve others' (1 Peter 4:10). The gifts we have received are not primarily for our own benefit. Because of this Paul can say, 'Each member belongs to all the others' (Romans 12:5).

In Ephesians 4 Paul says more about how the gifts are to be used for service. First, he says that God gives some gifts (apostle, prophet, evangelist, pastor and teacher) 'to equip his people for works of service' (v 12). In other words they help others to discover, nurture and use their own gifts. Then, having been enabled in this way, God's people use their gifts 'so that the body of Christ may be built up until we all reach unity in the faith and in the knowledge of the Son of God and become mature, attaining to the whole measure of the fulness of Christ' (vv 12-13). The body 'grows and builds itself up in love, as each part does its work' (v 16).

It is a wonderful picture: a mixture of spiritual gifts working in harmony so that we can serve one another and make the body of Christ more united, more mature, more holy and more loving. Spiritual gifts help the Church become more like Jesus.

Love is the key
When we understand that the various gifts of the Spirit come from God, that they are given by grace, not chosen by us or deserved, and that they are to serve others and not ourselves, then we begin to realise that every gift is important.

Charles Brookfield was an English actor in the late 19th century. In later life he suffered an attack of pleurisy and soon afterwards was mistakenly reported to have died. This meant he had the unusual opportunity to read his own obituary notices! One newspaper said, 'Never a great actor, he was invaluable in small parts.'[46]

Every gift is significant, so every person is important. The Church needs those who play the valuable small parts, as well as those with spectacular or high profile gifts. This understanding should leave no room for selfish ambition or pride in our own attributes or achievements. Neither should it allow us to think our gifts are insignificant compared with others, making us envious of them. Even so, the temptation is there! Perhaps that is why Paul is quick to point out the importance of love in connection with the exercise of spiritual gifts.

Paul concludes his exploration of gifts in 1 Corinthians 12 with the words, 'I will show you the most excellent way' (v 31). He then goes on in Chapter 13 to say that no matter how gifted he might be, if he does not have love his service is empty and meaningless. He then continues, 'I am nothing' (v 2) and 'I gain nothing' (v 3).

Without love it is so easy to envy another's gifts as well as to boast and feel proud about our own. But love 'does not envy, it does not boast, it is not proud' (v 4). With love we understand that our gifts are given for the service of others. As Paul says, following the passage on gifts in Romans 12, 'Be devoted to one another in love. Honour one another above yourselves' (v 10).

Love is the key that opens the door to the good and meaningful use of the gifts that God has given us. It is this love that makes our service sacrificial – an offering of our gifts back to God and an act of service to others.

As Albert Orsborn wrote:

> I must love thee, love must rule me,
> > Springing up and flowing forth
> From a childlike heart within me,
> > Or my work is nothing worth.
> Love with passion and with patience,
> > Love with principle and fire,
> Love with heart and mind and utterance,
> > Serving Christ my one desire.
>
> > > (*SASB* 672 v3)

—— *Reflection Five* ——

Serving

In Part Five there has been an emphasis on serving as something that every Christian does. It is not just those with the title of minister, or members of a church who have accepted a particular responsibility, who serve – we all serve because we belong to Christ and are called to follow the example of our Servant Lord.

- *Is there something in these chapters which has challenged your perceptions about serving?*
- *What practical outcome might this have for you?*

The song below, by Anna Laetitia Waring, provides a rich resource to help us think about Christian service in different ways. The starting point is an obedient faith in a loving Father God and patient acceptance that life will bring many changes and challenges. The writer asks for a 'thoughtful love' and the 'daily strength' to minister to others whatever their circumstances, however small the task. It is all for God's glory.

Verse 4 reveals the secret the writer has discovered – that true freedom is found in serving Christ: 'a life of self-renouncing love is one of liberty'. Verse 5 moves to a global perspective: 'Wherever in the world I am'. There is an echo of Paul's statement in Philippians 4:10-13 where the apostle testifies to 'being content' (v 12) in serving God in any and every situation.

- *Read and reflect on the song and on Philippians 4:10-13.*

> Father, I know that all my life
>   Is portioned out for me;
> The changes that will surely come
>   I do not fear to see;
> I ask thee for a patient mind,
>   Intent on pleasing thee.

On the Altar

> I ask thee for a thoughtful love,
>   Through constant watching, wise,
> To greet the glad with joyful smiles,
>   And wipe the weeping eyes;
> A heart at leisure from itself,
>   To soothe and sympathise.
>
> I ask thee for the daily strength
>   To none that ask denied,
> A mind to blend with outward life
>   While keeping at thy side;
> Content to fill a little space
>   If thou be glorified.
>
> In service which thy love appoints
>   There are no bonds for me;
> My secret heart is taught the truth
>   That makes thy children free:
> A life of self-renouncing love
>   Is one of liberty.
>
> Wherever in the world I am,
>   In whatsoe'er estate,
> I have a fellowship with hearts
>   To keep and cultivate,
> A work of lowly love to do
>   For him on whom I wait.
>
>   (*SASB* 750)

- *Spend some time in prayer allowing God to confirm your identity as his beloved child. Bring to him the attitudes that hold you back from serving. Offer your spiritual gifts that will enable you to serve with grace, in the spirit of Jesus.*

Part Six

Doing Good

*Do not forget to do good
and to share with others,
for with such sacrifices God is pleased.
(Hebrews 13:16)*

Chapter 21
Do-gooders

THERE was once a naughty boy whose mother told him to 'sit still and be good'. It was an impossible command – unless being good means doing nothing, which was possibly what his mother had in mind! But being good is more than simply doing nothing bad – it means actively doing good.

Goodness is a fruit of the Spirit (Galatians 5:22). As such it is a Spirit-inspired attitude that expresses itself in actions. It is a dynamic quality that only becomes real when it is done. In other words, goodness is as goodness does – and this active goodness is a sacrifice that God appreciates: 'Do not forget to do good and to share with others, for with such sacrifices God is pleased' (Hebrews 13:16).

Doing good properly
To be called a 'do-gooder' is not always a compliment! It can be an insult when it refers to those who meddle in other people's business, trying to help where help may not be needed and is not appreciated. Even if help is needed, do-gooders may go about it the wrong way, naively supposing that their well-intentioned efforts (if they are well intentioned) are of benefit. In fact, the wrong kind of help may not be helpful at all – it may be harmful.

This kind of inappropriate help is nothing new. The ancient Greek philosopher Theophrastus witnessed it in his day. Around 300 BC he wrote: 'In the proffered services of the busybody there is much of the affectation of kind-heartedness, and little efficient aid.' [47] By 'efficient aid' he meant effective help – doing good properly.

William Booth knew the importance of efficient aid. Late one night in December 1887, as he was travelling through central London, he saw some men sleeping rough. His son, Bramwell, recalled the conversation that took place the following morning:

'Bramwell,' he cried, when he caught sight of me, 'did you know that men slept out all night on the bridges?'

'Well, yes,' I replied, 'a lot of poor fellows, I suppose, do that.'

'Then you ought to be ashamed of yourself to have known it and to have done nothing for them!' he went on, vehemently.

I began to speak of the difficulties, burdened as we were already, of taking up all sorts of Poor Law work, and so forth. My father stopped me ...

'Go and do something!' he said. 'We must do something.'

'What can we do?'

'Get them a shelter!'

'That will cost money.'

'Well, that is your affair! Something must be done. Get hold of a warehouse and warm it, and find something to cover them. But mind, Bramwell, no coddling!' [48]

'No coddling!' That meant the homeless men were not to be treated like helpless objects of pity. They were to be given respect, a sense of independence and the opportunity to help themselves. This was an example of doing good properly.

The greatest example, of course, is that of Jesus. Peter said, 'You know... how God anointed Jesus of Nazareth with the Holy Spirit and power, and he went around doing good and healing all who were under the power of the devil, because God was with him' (Acts 10:38). When the writer to the Hebrews told his readers not to forget to do good as a sacrifice to God (13:16), he was probably thinking of Jesus. So, if we want to offer the sacrifice of doing good – and doing good properly – we need to follow his example.

Signs of the Kingdom

The first thing to understand is that Jesus was empowered by the Holy Spirit. This highlights the spiritual dimension to his acts of goodness. His miracles were important in themselves, because when he healed someone he was meeting a real need, but there was also a deeper significance. The miracles were evidence that the Kingdom of God was at work.

The Kingdom of God was the central message of Jesus. It was a message proclaimed in words and deeds. By his words he invited people to enter the Kingdom – to accept the gracious reign of God and live in obedience to him. By his deeds he showed people the powerful impact of the Kingdom. When blind people received their sight and lepers were healed it was evidence that the Kingdom of God had come in the person of Jesus. John's Gospel makes this clear when it calls the miracles 'signs' of the glory of God. A sign is something that points beyond itself. The good works of Jesus were signs pointing to the loving and powerful reality of God.

Signs of the grace of God
Just like Jesus, we need to rely on the power of the Spirit. That is the first lesson in doing good properly. Of course, it does not mean that Christians have a monopoly on doing good. We all know of sincere and concerned people who do not profess a faith but who do wonderful things for others. The question is – are their actions also signs of the Kingdom? In one sense the answer is 'no'. If non-Christians are not members of the Kingdom of God, then their good works do not demonstrate the lordship of Christ in their lives.

But in another sense the answer is 'yes'. The Spirit is at work in the world as well as in the Church, and there is such a thing as 'common grace'. This is the grace of God at work in all people, even those who do not know him. It is common grace that enables non-Christians to do good things. So, in this sense, whenever they do good, they are showing signs of the Kingdom of God – even though they may not recognise them as such. We should pray that their eyes will be opened to see these signs and respond with obedient faith in God. More than that, we should look out for these signs, because non-Christians sometimes have a lot to teach us. By common grace they may have identified needs and provided responses that we have missed.

No strings attached
The second lesson to learn is that good is only done properly when there are no strings attached.

There have been disturbing examples in Christian history of missionaries taking advantage of people's poverty by providing food and other benefits if they will convert to Christianity. This has sometimes produced so-called 'rice Christians' – people who have responded only because of the material benefits and whose faith has not always been genuine. Sadly, some Christians still think in a similar way, believing that doing good is only really worthwhile if it is a means of evangelism. To them, good deeds are like the bait on the hook to catch the fish.

This was not the way of Jesus. He responded to people's needs because they were needy, not as the bait on a hook. The better image is of a partnership. His good deeds and his preaching were partners together in the work of the Kingdom of God.

John Stott puts it this way:

> His words explained his works, and his works dramatized his words. Hearing and seeing, voice and vision, were joined. Each supported the other. [49]

Although we do good without asking for a spiritual response in return, we can hope and pray that God will be at work in people's hearts. Jesus said, 'Let your light shine before others, that they may see your good deeds and glorify your Father in Heaven' (Matthew 5:16).

We do good because there is a need for good to be done, with no strings attached. But as we do so – as we let our light shine – we can pray that something of God is revealed in what we do for people and that, because of this, they will turn towards him.

Chapter 22
Love in Action

ON A number of occasions Jesus was moved with compassion to do good. Once, when faced with a large crowd and realising how hungry they were, he said:

> I have compassion for these people; they have already been with me three days and have nothing to eat. I do not want to send them away hungry, or they may collapse on the way.
> (Matthew 15:32)

Then, from just a few loaves of bread and some fish he miraculously fed the crowd.

Another time, two blind men asked Jesus to heal them:

> Jesus had compassion on them and touched their eyes. Immediately they received their sight and followed him.
> (Matthew 20:34)

Compassion is an important motivation for our good deeds. As J.B. Phillips writes: 'Unless our service to other people springs from true concern and compassion for them, we can never rise above the level of the "do-gooder".' [50]

Compassion, sympathy and empathy

So, what is compassion? The Greek word translated 'compassion' means an emotional response, deep from the heart. It is pity or sympathy. At the beginning of the twentieth century a new word was coined to describe something more than sympathy – it was the word 'empathy'.

Sympathy is about feeling sorry for someone, whereas empathy is about imagining yourself in another person's situation. It is, perhaps, a more accurate description of the compassion we see in Jesus.

It involves both the imagination and the emotions. It is not just feeling *for* someone, it is feeling *with* them. Feelings are important, but the compassion of Jesus was more than that. Whenever he was moved with compassion he was also moved to action – to heal, to feed, to teach, to raise the dead. Not only was there sympathy – or empathy – there was also a desire to help.

There are times in our lives when we are moved by people's troubles. But if sympathy is our only response then it is not the kind of compassion shown by Jesus. Compassion means we not only feel for, and feel with, someone in need – we also do good for them.

Compassion and love

But there was more involved when Jesus did good. Not only was there compassion, there was also love. Love is different from compassion. Compassion is a feeling, but love is a force – a force directed towards the good of other people.

The Greek word used most often for 'love' in the New Testament is *agapē*. And as William Barclay wrote:

> This *agapē*, this Christian love, is not merely an emotional experience which comes to us unbidden and unsought; it is a deliberate principle of the mind, and a deliberate conquest and achievement of the will. [51]

Love involves wisdom and intention as well as emotion. The feeling of compassion may move us to do good for someone, but love helps us do what is wisest and best. A simple emotional reaction to a person in need could lead to an inappropriate response, whereas love, which involves heart, mind and will, enables us to think it through and do the greatest good for them. It was this kind of love that, as we saw earlier, led William Booth to respond to the sight of homeless men with not only the instruction, 'Go and do something!' but also, 'No coddling!'

Heart, mind and will worked together perfectly in the life of Jesus. He 'went around doing good' because compassion and love led him to act for the best. And it was this love that motivated his greatest act of good – the giving of his life for the salvation of the world.

Worthy of love

If doing good is motivated by love, it is important to think about why we ought to love people. Do we love them because they are lovable or have done something to deserve it? If so, where does that leave people who are not lovable and have done nothing to deserve it? There must be something about people that makes them worthy of love, no matter who they are or what they have done.

We only have to turn to the opening chapters of the Bible to find out what makes people worthy of love:

> So God created mankind in his own image,
> in the image of God he created them;
> male and female he created them.
>
> (Genesis 1:27)

People are worthy of love because they are made in the image of God. Clearly we are not images of God in a physical sense. But there are other ways in which we are Godlike:

- We have minds to think, reason and reflect.
- We can recognise moral values and make moral choices, even if they are not always the right ones.
- We are relational – able to love and be loved.
- We have been given dominion over God's creation.
- We are creative – able to innovate through art and science.
- We are spiritual – made for a relationship with God.

Because we are made in the image of God, we are of infinite worth – and are worthy of love. The psalmist makes a similar point:

> When I consider your heavens,
> the work of your fingers,
> the moon and the stars,
> which you have set in place,
> what is mankind that you are mindful of them,
> human beings that you care for them?
> You have made them a little lower than the angels
> and crowned them with glory and honour.
>
> (Psalm 8:3-5)

Why is it that God is mindful of us and cares for us? Because we are the crowning glory of his creation.

Over the centuries writers and philosophers have thought of

humankind in various ways. Thomas Carlyle, for example, described a human being as a 'two-legged animal without feathers'.[52] That might be true but it is not a very full description! Shakespeare's Hamlet says:

> What a piece of work is a man! How noble in reason, how infinite in faculty! In form and moving how express and admirable! In action how like an angel! In apprehension how like a god! [53]

If Hamlet highlights humankind's good points, Blaise Pascal was perhaps more realistic:

> What kind of freak is man! What a novelty he is, how absurd he is, how chaotic and what a mass of contradictions, and yet what a prodigy! He is judge of all things, yet a feeble worm. He is a repository of truth, and yet sinks into such doubt and error. He is the glory and the scum of the universe![54]

Pascal was right. Humanity is fallen, so we are a 'mass of contradictions', capable of great good and enormous evil. Nevertheless, everyone is made in the image of God, so is infinitely valuable and worthy of love.

A godly point of view

People do not always regard others as infinitely valuable. But Jesus does, and so must we. Paul wrote, 'From now on we regard no one from a worldly point of view' (2 Corinthians 5:16). Followers of Jesus are called to see people in a special way – to look past their unlovable characteristics and see the image of God in them. That is how God sees them. And it is this godly point of view that we should have.

The worldly point of view sees people very differently from the godly point of view. The worldly point of view regards them as objects to be exploited rather than people to be loved. This leads to evils such as human trafficking and modern slavery, which affect men, women and children who are used for sexual exploitation, forced labour and domestic servitude.

From a worldly point of view we can see people as competitors, to be outdone and looked down on if they fail to achieve as much as we do. From a godly point of view every person is equal in God's sight and everyone's contribution to society is to be valued.

The worldly point of view deals in stereotypes such as race, nationality, gender, class and age – and treats people differently as a result. The godly point of view sees people as unique individuals, worthy of respect and to be treated equally.

A good example of someone with this godly point of view is Trevor Huddleston, an English Anglican priest who served in South Africa in the 1940s. As a child Desmond Tutu met him and remembers how different that was from his experience of a white person with a worldly point of view:

> One of the earliest and most painful memories of my childhood is accompanying my father, a school principal, to the shop – I think it was in Ventersdorp – and witnessing him being humiliated by a young white shop assistant… being addressed, 'Ja, boy?' by one much younger than himself, and being forced to swallow his pride.
>
> But I believe the most defining moment of my life occurred when I was about nine years old, outside the Blind Institute in Roodepoort where my mother was a domestic worker. We were standing on the stoep when this tall white man in a black cassock, and a hat, swept by. I did not know that it was Trevor Huddleston. He doffed his hat in greeting my mother.
>
> I was relatively stunned at the time, but only later came to realise the extent to which it had blown my mind that a white man would doff his hat to my mother. It was something I could never have imagined. The impossible was possible.
>
> I subsequently discovered that this was quite consistent with Trevor Huddleston's theology: that every person is of significance, of infinite value, because they are created in the image of God. [55]

Worldly eyes see the outward appearance and fail to recognise a person's true worth. From a godly point of view people are precious individuals, worthy of the love that arouses compassion and responds with acts of goodness.

Chapter 23
Social Justice

WHEN Catherine Booth was a girl of just nine she saw 'a manifestly drunken lout being dragged along by a policeman'. Close behind was a noisy crowd of youths, jeering and laughing. Catherine walked alongside the man, holding his hand all the way to the police station, assuring him that there was at least one person prepared to treat him with kindness. At that moment, as there would be all through her life, there was 'a hot spring of indignation in her, ready to leap up in the presence of cruelty or injustice'. [56]

In responding this way, Catherine was reflecting something of the nature of Jesus. If compassion was a powerful emotion at work in his life, so was the closely related emotion of anger. An incident in Jerusalem shows this clearly. Jesus entered the Temple courts and saw the merchants and money-changers. It made him angry: 'He overturned the tables of the money-changers and the benches of those selling doves' (Matthew 21:12). Jesus reacted this way because what was happening was wrong – people were being exploited.

Injustice
The incident took place in the outer court of the Temple, the Court of the Gentiles, where pilgrims from any nation could come to pray. This court had become a busy, noisy marketplace instead of 'a house of prayer for all nations' (Mark 11:17).

The money-changers were there so that worshippers could change their money into a half-shekel, which was the annual Temple tax. No other coin was acceptable to the authorities. The trouble was that the money-changers charged almost 30 per cent commission for the exchange. And if the coin the worshippers wanted to change was worth more than a half-shekel, they could only get their change if they paid double the commission, which amounted to half a day's wages for a working man. It was an unjustified and an unjust financial penalty.

There were other crooked practices in the Temple court. Worshippers who came to make a sacrifice had to be sure their sacrificial dove was perfect. If they brought one into the Temple they had to pay an inspector to examine it and ran the risk of it being rejected as imperfect. Alternatively, they could buy a dove that had already passed the inspection from a seller inside the Temple, but the price was much higher than those on sale outside. Either way the worshipper was penalised.

Worshippers were faced with crowds, noise and crooked practices. No wonder Jesus called the Temple 'a den of robbers' (Mark 11:17); no wonder he became angry and drove them out. William Barclay wrote:

> Jesus' ejection of the money changers and the sellers of doves demonstrates his passion for social justice. His anger was kindled to a white heat at the sight of simple people cheated, swindled and imposed upon by clever and rapacious scoundrels.[57]

There were other occasions when Jesus was angry at injustice. Early in his ministry he entered a synagogue where he met a man with a shrivelled hand (Mark 3:1-6). Some in the crowd were looking for a reason to accuse Jesus and thought this was the perfect opportunity. He might heal the man, then they could accuse him of working on the Sabbath. Jesus challenged them with a question:

> 'Which is lawful on the Sabbath: to do good or to do evil, to save life or to kill?' But they remained silent.
>
> (v 4)

His response?

> He looked around at them in anger and, deeply distressed at their stubborn hearts, said to the man, 'Stretch out your hand.' He stretched it out, and his hand was completely restored.
>
> (v 5)

Jesus was angry because they could see no reason to help and heal the man on the Sabbath. They put their regulations before the man's need – and that was unjust. Jesus put things right and healed him.

Jesus was also angry when people were overlooked and excluded. On one occasion people tried to bring their small children to him so he could bless them (Mark 10:13-16). The disciples stopped them, perhaps thinking that he was too tired or too busy to see the children. But when

Jesus noticed this 'he was indignant'. To Jesus, children were important – indeed, they were examples to be followed when it came to entering the Kingdom. So, he became angry when they were excluded from his presence.

Selfless anger
Injustice made Jesus indignant. But was this an appropriate response? After all, Paul said, love 'is not easily angered' (1 Corinthians 13:5). Anger is not good if it is selfish, and presumably this is what Paul had in mind – the kind of anger that erupts when our personal interests are threatened, or the anger that is laced with spite and bitterness. Someone once said that anger is 'our pride coming to the rescue of our reputation'.

But that was not the anger that Jesus displayed. He was indignant because other people's interests were threatened. His anger was selfless, not selfish – righteous, not self-righteous. It was what Barclay calls 'the wrath of a pure love'. [58]

When Jesus saw people in need it seems that his primary emotion was compassion, and it moved him to deal with their problems. But when he saw injustice his primary emotion was anger, which motivated him to remove the cause of their problems. His compassion and his anger were evidence of his deep feeling for people in need. Both emotions were motivated, and channelled into action, by pure love.

Follow justice
If we want to follow the example of Jesus we will help and support people in need. This could mean simply offering someone a listening ear or a helping hand. It might involve giving a wise or encouraging word, because words can also be good deeds. Or it may involve supporting organisations that do good works. Helping people is good but it is not always good enough. We also need to ask why people are in need – and try to tackle the causes.

Deuteronomy 16:20 says, 'Follow justice and justice alone.' This call comes near the end of a chapter that outlines the three annual sacrificial festivals we looked at in Chapter Two. The message is clear – worship and justice belong together. The Hebrew word translated as 'justice' in this verse is *tzedek*. It means putting wrongs right and includes the ideas of fairness, uprightness and equity. The Old Testament regards it as an attribute of God and a requirement for his people.

Justice may involve speaking up for those who are not heard or enabling them to speak up for themselves. It could mean acting for those who have no power over their circumstances by confronting crooked, ignorant or powerful people and challenging unjust practices and systems. There is no shortage of issues to tackle: human trafficking, prejudice, corruption, unfair trade, the abuse of vulnerable people, to name just a few.

Someone once said, 'Sometimes I would like to ask God why he allows poverty, suffering and injustice, when he could do something about it. But I'm afraid he would ask me the same question.'

He does! And this Franciscan benediction gives us an idea of how we need to respond to that question:

> May God bless you with discomfort
> At easy answers, half-truths and superficial relationships,
> So that you may live deep within your heart.
>
> May God bless you with anger
> At injustice, oppression and the exploitation of people,
> So that you may work for justice, freedom and peace.
>
> May God bless you with tears
> To shed for those who suffer pain, rejection, hunger and war,
> So that you may reach out your hand to comfort them and
> To turn their pain into joy.
>
> And may God bless you with enough foolishness
> To believe that you can make a difference in the world,
> So that you can do what others claim cannot be done
> To bring justice and kindness to all our children and the poor. [59]

Chapter 24
Sacrificial Good

WE are thinking about doing good as a sacrifice. In the parable of the good Samaritan (Luke 10) Jesus helps us see what sacrificial good looks like.

The parable was told in response to a question from a religious lawyer. If the greatest commandment is to love God wholeheartedly and to love your neighbour as yourself, then, asked the lawyer, 'who is my neighbour?' In response Jesus told the story of a man who was attacked and robbed on the road between Jerusalem and Jericho. Neither the priest nor the Levite who came along stopped to help. Instead, it was the Samaritan who 'took pity on him' and responded. Jesus asked the lawyer, 'Which of these three do you think was a neighbour to the man who fell into the hands of robbers?' The lawyer answered, 'The one who had mercy on him.' Jesus commanded him, 'Go and do likewise.'

Giving up preconceptions
If we are to do likewise we need to realise what doing good meant for this Samaritan. It was a costly act and a risky act.

The initial cost was to his established perceptions and prejudices. He was a Samaritan and the victim was a Jew. There had been 300 years of hostility between Samaritans and Jews. This needed to be laid to one side. He had to look past differences of belief and culture to simply see a man in need.

Jesus challenged his hearers to do the same. We tend to forget how shocking this story must have been to those Jews who first heard it. They would have found it hard enough to imagine a Jew taking pity on a Samaritan, but for a Samaritan to take pity on a Jew? That was beyond belief! It was this startling thought that challenged their preconceptions.

Doing sacrificial good means giving up our preconceived ideas, which are sometimes faulty or prejudiced, gaining an insight into a person's need and doing something about it. Jesus said, 'In everything, do to others what you would have them do to you' (Matthew 7:12). When we look at others from this perspective, we see how we would like to be treated if we were in their position – and that should lead us to act accordingly.

Taking risks
The Samaritan also took a physical risk in helping the man on the road. The Jew had been attacked and robbed – the same could happen to the Samaritan if he stopped to help. What if the robbers were lying in wait for another traveller? But human need outweighed any thought for his own safety.

Paul speaks of Epaphroditus 'who risked his life' in the work of Christ (Philippians 2:25-30). The word translated 'risked' comes from a root that means 'to throw down a stake'. [60] It is the language of gambling. This idea was taken up in the fourth century to refer to a group of Christians who risked their lives in nursing the sick and burying the dead during dangerous epidemics. They were called 'Gamblers'.

Most of our good deeds do not carry such a risk, but if they do, we need to consider whether the good we can do justifies the risk we face. For example, putting ourselves at risk by picking up a hitchhiker when we are travelling alone is not always wise. The situation might be different if we stopped to assist someone injured in an accident.

Sacrificing resources
Unlike Epaphroditus it is unlikely that we will need to risk our lives in doing good but we can sometimes be called to sacrifice our resources. The Samaritan may have had important business elsewhere but he gave his time and energy to care for the man in need. He also made a financial sacrifice. Not only did he pay for the injured man to stay at the inn, he also promised to cover any extra expense that was incurred while he was away. He made this commitment not knowing how much it would cost, so risked paying out more than he could afford.

We also might be called on to commit more than we expect or can comfortably give. Time, effort and money – these are some of the costs involved in doing good.

Facing misunderstanding

There may be other, less tangible costs. Imagine if the Samaritan's friends and family heard about his actions. Would they have understood and supported him, or criticised him for helping someone of a hated race and religion? Good deeds can attract misunderstanding. Our reputation can be put at risk. It happened to Jesus when he was criticised by respectable people for mixing with the despised tax collectors and prostitutes. Sometimes misunderstanding is part of the cost of caring. More likely it comes if we take a stand for social justice. Archbishop Hélder Câmara, of Brazil, said:

> When I give food to the poor, they call me a saint. When I ask why they are poor, they call me a communist. [61]

Why is God pleased?

Romans 12:1 says the offering of ourselves as a living sacrifice is 'holy and pleasing to God'. Hebrews 13:16 tells us that when we turn that commitment into practical action he is also pleased.

Why is this so? God is pleased because, in doing good, we are loving and valuing people whom he loves and values. We are helping to bring something of his Kingdom into the world – helping to defeat the evil that threatens people for whom he cares.

Doing good pleases God because it is a sign that we have not taken his goodness for granted. We have recognised what he has done for us. Our response is not only to praise and thank him but also to reflect his goodness to others in the things we say and do: 'Dear friends, since God so loved us, we also ought to love one another' (1 John 4:11). Just as Old Testament sacrifices were responses to the grace of God, so are the sacrifices of doing good.

Finally, God is pleased because when we do good to others we are serving Jesus. As Jesus said in the parable of the sheep and the goats in Matthew 25, when we feed the hungry, give the thirsty something to drink, invite the stranger in, clothe those who need clothes and visit those who are ill or in prison, we do it to him. Jesus so identifies with the suffering of humankind, and feels that suffering as if it were his own, that the good we do for others is accepted as an expression of our love for him. So, 'do not forget to do good and to share with others, for with such sacrifices God is pleased' (Hebrews 13:16).

—— Reflection Six ——

Doing Good

- *As a starting point for this reflection, think about the word 'good' and the ways in which it is used... How do you define 'good'?*

The word 'good' on its own is often used to express approval, to denote that something has been done well or has had a pleasing outcome. It can define the quality of an action, person or object. It was used in the very beginning to describe the results of God's activity in creation. 'God saw that it was good' is the constant refrain in Genesis Chapter One as each aspect of creation is brought into being.

The writer of Proverbs advises, 'Do not withhold good from those to whom it is due, when it is in your power to act' (3:27). To do something or to give something good is portrayed as an active choice, a decision that people are empowered to make.

- *What comes to mind when you think about 'doing good'? Can you make a link between human activity and God's creative activity, if we think of our actions as the expression of our spiritual experience?*

Doing good is an integral part of living in relationship with our Father God. We see this very clearly in the life of Jesus. When Peter shared the gospel with Cornelius and his household at Joppa, he simply said that Jesus 'went around doing good ... because God was with him' (Acts 10:38).

The writer to the Hebrews reminds the Christians to whom he is writing, 'And do not forget to do good and to share with others, for with such sacrifices God is pleased' (13:16). The opposite of 'doing good' is not necessarily 'doing bad', but in this context it is probably 'doing nothing' and being selfish. A simple act of kindness or a gift which could make such a difference to another person is portrayed as a 'sacrifice', an offering which is pleasing to God.

On the Altar

There may be a tendency to think of 'doing good' in terms of special projects taking place in other parts of the world to relieve human suffering. We greatly admire people who go and devote themselves to such work but may not feel that we can do very much. Yet the challenge comes to all Christians to turn compassion into action. We do not act because we are motivated by recognition or results but because 'Christ's love compels us' (2 Corinthians 5:14).

- *Has something you have read or thought about in Part Six challenged your understanding of 'doing good'? If you have been inspired to do something, write it down, with today's date, and keep it where you will be reminded of your resolve.*

Part Seven

Giving

I am amply supplied, now that I have received from Epaphroditus the gifts you sent. They are a fragrant offering, an acceptable sacrifice, pleasing to God.
(Philippians 4:18)

Chapter 25
A Spiritual Issue

A NUMBER of years ago the letters page of a Salvation Army periodical included some correspondence about giving. One writer referred to the question of whether the money given during worship should be called the 'collection' or the 'offering'. He told of an occasion in one corps when the corps sergeant-major announced, 'Your offering will now be received.' The divisional commander was leading the meeting that Sunday and responded, 'This is The Salvation Army and in the Army we have a collection, not an offering.' The corps sergeant-major turned again to the congregation and said, 'Whatever we call it in the Army, we hope you will regard it as your offering to God, not as the Army collecting something from you.'[62] A few weeks later another letter writer commented: 'Salvationists take up an offering, binmen make a collection!'[63]

Actually, both terms are biblical. In Philippians 4:18 Paul speaks of 'a fragrant offering' and in 1 Corinthians 16:1 he mentions 'the collection for the Lord's people'. Whether it is a collection or an offering might depend on whether you are giving or receiving. Those receiving the money, or passing round the plate, would say they are taking up the collection – those who are giving would say they are making an offering. The receivers could also say they are collecting the offering and the givers could say they are giving their offering to the collection! So, it really does not matter what we call our giving, as long as we give.

The giving we will think about in these chapters can include giving to the Church for its spiritual and social work, giving to charities or agencies – Christian and non-Christian – and giving to individuals. All can represent our giving to God.

Not everyone likes being asked to give. Some think that what they do with their money is their business. They are right. It is their business, but it is also God's business. That is why Jesus had so much to say about money and how we use it. To him it was a spiritual issue. Jesus knew that a total commitment to material prosperity was incompatible with a total commitment to God. He was clear about it:

> No one can serve two masters. Either you will hate the one and love the other, or you will be devoted to the one and despise the other. You cannot serve both God and Money.
>
> (Matthew 6:24)

The love of money

This does not mean money is a bad thing – although some people think the Bible says this. They quote the words, 'Money is the root of all evil'. But this is inaccurate. The Bible actually says, 'The love of money is a root of all kinds of evil' (1 Timothy 6:10) – and it warns us: 'Keep your lives free from the love of money and be content with what you have' (Hebrews 13:5).

Money itself is not bad, but the love of money is. Money is neither good nor bad but it can attract our love, our devotion and our service. When it does that, our relationship with it is unhealthy, even dangerous.

In the parable of the sower, Jesus pointed out that 'the deceitfulness of wealth' can damage our faith (Matthew 13:22). Wealth can deceive us by making us think it provides security and contentment. An Old Testament proverb gives the same message:

> Do not wear yourself out to get rich;
>   do not trust your own cleverness.
> Cast but a glance at riches, and they are gone,
>   for they will surely sprout wings
>   and fly off to the sky like an eagle.
>
> (Proverbs 23:4-5)

If we put our trust in money it may fail us – and it can harm us if it becomes more important to us than God is.

Treasures in Heaven

Christians are members of the Kingdom of God. We are under God's rule and should be responsive to his will in every area of our lives. How we use our financial resources is one measure of how far we have come under his rule. Few things are more spiritual than our attitude towards money.

Martin Luther said: 'Three conversions are necessary: conversion of the heart, the mind and the purse.'[64] Our financial commitment is a gauge of our spiritual commitment. We cannot separate the two. How we use our money – or anything that God gives us – has eternal consequences. Jesus said:

> Do not store up for yourselves treasures on earth, where moths and vermin destroy, and where thieves break in and steal. But store up for yourselves treasures in heaven, where moths and vermin do not destroy, and where thieves do not break in and steal.
> (Matthew 6:19-20)

How do we store up 'treasures in Heaven'? Jesus said:

> Sell your possessions and give to the poor. Provide purses for yourselves that will not wear out, a treasure in heaven that will never fail, where no thief comes near and no moth destroys.
> (Luke 12:33)

Jesus emphasised giving. But he was not saying we can buy a place in Heaven by being generous on Earth. Rather, the way we give our money is a sign of our priorities – whether we put God first or possessions first. It is this that has eternal consequences.

Paul followed Jesus' example and put money into its spiritual context. He called the gifts he received from the Philippians 'a fragrant offering, an acceptable sacrifice, pleasing to God' (Philippians 4:18).

Giving is part of worship – one aspect of the 'true and proper worship' that is involved in giving ourselves as 'a living sacrifice' (Romans 12:1). When we see giving in this way it changes our money from being a potential rival to God into being a servant of God.

Chapter 26
Generous and Costly

WHEN Paul wrote to the Philippians he thanked them for their generosity. He had been 'amply supplied' (Philippians 4:18) – and not for the first time. Earlier in his ministry they had given to him 'more than once' (v 16).

They gave generously without expecting anything in return, which is surprising when you consider where they came from. Philippi was in Macedonia, part of the Gentile world with a Greek culture. In that world this kind of giving was highly unusual.

Giving to the poor
The Gentile world and the Jewish world were both divided into three socio-economic groups: each had a wealthy élite, a small middle class and a large population of poor people. The big difference was how these two worlds regarded their giving to the poor.

In Palestine, poverty was so widespread that many people relied on handouts. Fortunately for them, the idea of giving to the poor was deeply embedded in Jewish culture. Throughout the Old Testament, God was seen as the protector of the poor, and God's people were expected to care for them. In the first century AD this was expressed in almsgiving – the giving of money to the poor by individuals, households and religious groups. It was given freely, with no strings attached.

By contrast, giving in the Gentile world definitely did have strings attached! Instead of almsgiving there was the custom of patronage, which involved an exchange of goods or services between people of unequal status, such as a master and a freedman. This kind of giving was practised with a view to receiving something in return. The benefactor was also a beneficiary.

As a missionary to the Gentiles, Paul brought with him the Jewish idea of giving. The Philippians must have learnt well, because this is just what they practised when they sent gifts to help him. It was not patronage. They could expect nothing in return, because Paul had nothing to give them. They were simply being generous.

Generous giving does, of course, have its dangers. There is the possibility that people will become dependent and not feel the need to try and improve their own situation. After all, if someone is generous enough to keep providing for you, why provide for yourself? This takes us back to the idea of the do-gooder in Chapter 21, whose help can do more harm than good. True generosity will not ask for anything back personally but will give with the expectation that recipients will, if possible, try to help themselves. It is a hand up rather than a handout. It should not create dependency.

Giving and receiving
Even though no personal gain should be expected when we give, Paul reminds the Philippians that they will indeed receive something back. He says, 'Not that I desire your gifts; what I desire is that more be credited to your account' (Philippians 4:17). Paul does not mean they will receive money in return for the money they give. This was not an early version of the 'prosperity gospel' that we sometimes hear promoted today, and which wrongly teaches that if you have enough faith and you give your money to God's work, you are guaranteed greater material wealth in return. It was nothing like that. Paul was simply reminding them that because they were generous givers God would bless them. Perhaps Paul had the words of Jesus in mind: 'It is more blessed to give than to receive' (Acts 20:35). The same thought is expressed in an old Welsh proverb, 'The greatest joy in giving is to be the one who gives.'

Beyond generosity
While this is true, it is not actually the money we give that attracts God's blessing. Our generous giving is simply a sign of a generous and faithful heart – and it is because of this that God blesses us. Sometimes this blessing will be material but more often it will be spiritual – the blessing of peace, contentment and joy.

Generosity is commendable but – depending on our circumstances – it may not actually cost us very much. Sometimes we need to go

Generous and Costly

beyond generous giving towards costly giving. In this way the giving of money closely resembles Old Testament sacrifices. Both involve giving something tangible and of real cost to us.

Jesus pointed out an example of costly giving when he noticed a poor widow putting 'two very small copper coins' into the Temple treasury (Mark 12:41-44). He said:

> This poor widow has put more into the treasury than all the others. They all gave out of their wealth; but she, out of her poverty, put in everything – all she had to live on.

The wealthy givers may have been generous but, though the widow gave less, her giving was costly.

The translators of the *New International Version (NIV)* have done something intriguing with these verses. The original Greek text uses the same verb for the action of both the rich givers and the poor widow. It is the verb *ballō*, which means 'to cast into', 'to throw' or 'to put into'. The *NIV* has used these different possible translations to make a distinction between the ways the people in this story gave their money. Whereas the rich people (v 41) 'threw in' their offering, suggesting a careless, casual approach to giving – the widow 'put in' hers, suggesting a careful, worshipful attitude. The way these verses have been translated reveals the true spirit of costly giving.

The attitude of renunciation

Jesus calls all his disciples to costly giving. For some it means giving up everything. Peter, James and John 'left everything and followed him' (Luke 5:11). There was a similar challenge to a rich ruler. Jesus said, 'Sell everything you have and give to the poor, and you will have treasure in Heaven. Then come, follow me' (Luke 18:18-22). Sadly, the man was not prepared to accept the challenge.

Not every would-be disciple is expected to do this. It is true that Jesus said, 'Those of you who do not give up everything you have cannot be my disciples' (Luke 14:33), but it is also true that not everyone responded literally – and not everyone was expected to. Mary and Martha were disciples of Jesus but they did not even leave their home, let alone give it up. And when Zacchaeus was saved he gave half his possessions to the poor and paid back four times the amount he had cheated people – but he did not give up everything.

What Jesus is really calling for is an *attitude* of renunciation. For some, this will mean giving up everything to follow. Others will be expected to have a willingness to give everything, rather than actually giving everything. As I. H. Marshall says: 'The disciple must be continually ready (present tense) to give up all that he has got in order to follow Jesus.' [65]

All for Jesus
Even though not all the disciples gave up everything, they were prepared to do so if necessary. And one way this was expressed was in their willingness to put their possessions at the disposal of Jesus. So, Mary and Martha hosted Jesus and the other disciples in their home. And in the Early Church in Jerusalem this willingness was shown by making their possessions available to one another:

> All the believers were one in heart and mind. No one claimed that any of their possessions was their own, but they shared everything they had. With great power the apostles continued to testify to the resurrection of the Lord Jesus. And God's grace was so powerfully at work in them all that there was no needy person among them. For from time to time those who owned land or houses sold them, brought the money from the sales and put it at the apostles' feet, and it was distributed to anyone who had need.
>
> (Acts 4:32-35)

Jesus said, 'Whoever wants to be my disciple must deny themselves and take up their cross daily and follow me' (Luke 9:23). This is the basic call to discipleship. To deny ourselves is to give up our right to call anything our own. It is to recognise that everything we have has come from God and is to be used for him. Being willing to do this – making all we have available to God – is an important form of costly giving.

Chapter 27
Counting the Cost

IS it possible to define or quantify costly giving? The Old Testament certainly gives that impression. There, the standard of giving was the tithe – one tenth (10 per cent). The command is in Leviticus 27:30:

> A tithe of everything from the land, whether grain from the soil or fruit from the trees, belongs to the LORD; it is holy to the LORD.

The prophet Malachi tells the people that to give anything less than this is to rob God (Malachi 3:8). On the other hand, if they obey God's command they will be richly blessed:

> 'Bring the whole tithe into the storehouse, that there may be food in my house. Test me in this,' says the LORD Almighty, 'and see if I will not throw open the floodgates of heaven and pour out so much blessing that there will not be room enough to store it'.
> (Malachi 3:10)

Old Testament tithing began as a tenth of all crops but developed to include cattle and finally applied to all income. New Testament believers from a Jewish background would have been aware of the importance of tithing and would have practised it. Indeed, Jesus endorsed it. He criticised the teachers of the Law and the Pharisees for paying their tithe while not concerning themselves with 'more important matters of the law – justice, mercy and faithfulness' (Matthew 23:23). In doing so he was not saying that these are alternatives. He went on to say both were expected: 'You should have practised the latter, without neglecting the former.' Jesus expected them to tithe.

Paul does not mention tithing, but probably had it in mind when he wrote about proportionate giving:

> On the first day of every week, each one of you should set aside a sum of money in keeping with your income.
> (1 Corinthians 16:2)

A minimum standard

If tithing is the Old Testament standard, then for Christians it should perhaps be the minimum. We are called to generous and costly giving, and a strict tithe does not always answer that call. Clearly, 10 per cent for people on a high income will be less costly in real terms than 10 per cent for people on a lower income.

A Texas millionaire called Robert Gilmour Le Tourneau recognised the need to go beyond the tithe, because for him there would be no real cost in giving just 10 per cent. He said:

> The question is not how much of my money I give to God, but rather how much of God's money I keep. [66]

His response to that question was to give 90 per cent of the assets of his manufacturing business to his Christian foundation, as well as 90 per cent of the income from the remaining share of the business. This did not make him poor – but it was an expression of generous and costly giving.

Few Christians will be able to follow Le Tourneau's example, but the question he posed is still relevant. How much of God's money should we keep? Some have answered this by practising the 'graduated tithe'. Ronald Sider describes how this worked for him and his wife:

> When Arbutus and I decided to adopt a graduated scale for our giving in 1969, we started by sitting down and trying to calculate honestly what we would need to live for a year. We wanted a figure that would permit reasonable comfort but not all the luxuries ... Somehow we arrived at a figure of $7,000 ... We decided to continue paying a tithe of 10 per cent on this basic amount. Then for every additional thousand dollars of income above the basic amount, we decided to increase our giving by five per cent on that thousand. [67]

Ronald Sider regards this as a modest approach to giving. In fact, he says it is 'probably so modest that it verges on unfaithfulness to Saint Paul'. Nevertheless, it is 'sufficiently radical that its implementation would revolutionize the ministry and life of the Church!' [68]

The graduated tithe is not how everyone will want to calculate their costly giving but it is one idea of how it could be done. And there will naturally be questions such as: 'Should I work out my tithe or graduated giving before or after tax?' and 'Should all my giving be to the Church or can giving to other causes be included in my tithe or graduated giving?' Each individual must answer those questions for themself.

Fair trade
Another way to count the cost of giving could involve thinking carefully about what we buy and where we buy it from. If we choose to buy fairly traded goods we may pay a little more but we will be helping to create better working conditions and fairer incomes for workers in developing countries.

One example of fair trade is The Salvation Army's 'Others' brand, which has the motto 'trade for hope'. It provides opportunities for people in developing countries to produce items such as kitchen goods, textiles, bags, cards and note pads.

Some fair trade organisations produce tea, coffee and other food items. Speaking at an exhibition of fairly traded goods at The Salvation Army's International Headquarters in 2014, the Managing Director of Others, Jan Aasman Størksen, said he hoped people would think beyond the 'buy one, get one free' culture and instead seek to spend their money wisely – even sacrificially – to support people in the developing world.

Beyond calculation
Thinking carefully about our giving – whether in tithing or trading – is important, but it is not the whole story. Irenaeus, an influential bishop of the second century, made it clear that responding to God by careful calculation alone is not sufficient. He said:

> Sacrifices there were among the people [of Israel]; sacrifices there are, too, in the Church …They [the Jews] had indeed the tithes of their goods consecrated to him [God], but those who have received liberty set aside all their possessions for the Lord's purposes, bestowing joyfully and freely …[69]

His point was that giving is no longer a duty but a voluntary act of devotion, so Christians should not limit their giving to a tithe. We do need to think it through carefully, but there should also be freedom and joy in our giving – and this is what we will look at in the next chapter.

Chapter 28
Cheerful Giving

IT is possible for us to give simply because we are expected to. Even costly giving can be done out of a sense of duty. But this is far from the New Testament picture of sacrificial giving where we see money given, not grudgingly but gladly in the way Paul recommends:

> Each of you should give what you have decided in your heart to give, not reluctantly or under compulsion, for God loves a cheerful giver.
> (2 Corinthians 9:7)

This does not mean that we should only give when we feel happy about it! It means we are glad about doing what we know we should do.

Overflowing joy
Paul explains cheerful giving in 2 Corinthians Chapters 8 and 9. He begins by using the example of those in the Macedonian churches, who had given money to support the church in Jerusalem. The most important thing he highlights is that they 'gave themselves first of all to the Lord, and then by the will of God also to us' (8:5). They had offered themselves as a living sacrifice to God, and the sacrifice of their giving was a result of this. Only when we have offered ourselves to God is giving transformed from duty into devotion. Then, instead of asking ourselves 'How much *should* we give?' we ask 'How much *can* we give?'

The Macedonian churches gave sacrificially but also so joyfully and spontaneously that Paul can say, 'In the midst of a very severe trial, their overflowing joy and their extreme poverty welled up in rich generosity' (8:2). They did not regard it as a burden. They saw it as a privilege and were glad to give:

> ...they gave as much as they were able, and even beyond their ability. Entirely on their own, they urgently pleaded with us for the privilege of sharing in this service to the Lord's people.
> (8:3-4)

At the root of all this was the boundless generosity of Jesus:

> For you know the grace of our Lord Jesus Christ, that though he was rich, yet for your sake he became poor, so that you through his poverty might become rich.
>
> (8:9)

Not only was Jesus the example of sacrificial giving, he was also the inspiration for cheerful giving. Paul says the Corinthians could give gladly because of all Jesus had done for them.

Their giving was an expression of their thanks to God 'for his indescribable gift!' (9:15). Sacrificial giving is thanksgiving – an act of joyous gratitude to God who so loved the world that he gave his one and only Son.

Contentment

Paul tells the Philippians that their gifts are 'a fragrant offering, an acceptable sacrifice' (4:18). He had already said something about his own attitude to money and possessions a few verses earlier:

> I know what it is to be in need, and I know what it is to have plenty. I have learnt the secret of being content in any and every situation, whether well fed or hungry, whether living in plenty or in want.
>
> (4:12)

Wealth meant very little to Paul. He could take it or leave it. He was content with it or without it. This sense of contentment is closely linked to the joy and peace that he mentions in the same chapter.

> Rejoice in the Lord always. I will say it again: rejoice! Let your gentleness be evident to all. The Lord is near. Do not be anxious about anything, but in every situation, by prayer and petition, with thanksgiving, present your requests to God. And the peace of God, which transcends all understanding, will guard your hearts and your minds in Christ Jesus.
>
> (4:4-7)

Contentment, rejoicing, lack of anxiety, thanksgiving and peace – all are part of a prayerful, trusting relationship with the Lord who 'is near'. In this relationship, and with these qualities, we can give cheerfully.

We will not be desperate to hold on to our money. We will not worry if we give sacrificially. We are content and we are joyful.

Richard Foster describes this attitude beautifully and paints a wonderful picture of a life not enslaved by material things – a life free from an anxious, grasping attitude, able to use money and possessions without being possessed by them. He writes:

> When we have a spirit of thanksgiving we can hold all things lightly. We receive; we do not grab. And when it is time to let go, we do so freely. We are not owners, only stewards. Our lives do not consist of the things that we have, for we live and move and breathe in God, not things. And may I add that this includes those intangible 'things' that are often our greatest treasures – status, reputation, position. These things come and go in life, and we can learn to be thankful when they come and thankful when they go. [70]

Spiritual vitality

Such freedom is a sign of spiritual vitality and devotion – and the generosity that it produces is expressed in more than just the giving of money.

We can be generous in giving our time and our talents, as well as our treasure, as John Gowans' poem 'Extravagance' makes clear:

> Please let me be extravagant
>   In what I give or do.
> I want to spend my 'Everything'
>   And all my time for you.
>
> If, feeling sorry for myself,
>   I start to count the cost,
> Then I shall be the poorer –
>   What I've gained will all be lost.
>
> Not penny-pinching, miserly,
>   Not keeping strict account;
> Investing all I have and then
>   Forgetting the amount!

On the Altar

> O Lord, when I begin to stray
> From dedication's track,
> Remind me of the way you gave,
> And I'll hold nothing back! [71]

This poem hints at the greatest act of giving – the self-giving of Jesus on the Cross. Any generosity of ours is a response to his generosity, his grace. In this way our sacrifice of giving reflects the Old Testament sacrifices, which, as we saw in Chapter Two, were a grateful response to the grace and mercy of God. We give because he gave – and continues to give.

── *Reflection Seven* ──

Giving

Here are some statements on the theme of giving based on the chapters you have just read:

Giving is a spiritual issue.
Our financial commitment is a measure of our spiritual commitment.
Giving is part of worship.

- *What do you think of these statements about giving? How do you respond?*

Generosity to the poor is a normal practice for God's people.
Generosity should not create dependency.
Generosity is the sign of a faithful heart.

- *Do you agree with these statements? Do they challenge you in any way?*

Giving should be costly and sacrificial.
Jesus is calling for an attitude of renunciation.
Willing obedience is one form of costly giving.

- *Do you agree with these statements? Do they challenge you in any way?*

- *Let the verses overleaf, taken from Brindley Boon's 'Dedication Song' written in connection with his commissioning as a Salvation Army officer, lead into moments of prayer, asking God to direct you personally in your giving.*

On the Altar

> Time, health and talents presenting,
>   All that I have shall be thine;
> Heart, mind and will consecrating,
>   No longer shall they be mine.
>
> O for a heart of compassion,
>   Moved at the impulse of love,
> Lost ones to bring to thy footstool,
>   Thy gracious riches to prove!
>
> *Take thou my life, Lord,*
>   *In deep submission I pray,*
> *My all to thee dedicating,*
>   *Accept my offering today.*

(*SASB* 591, vv 3, 4 and chorus)

Part Eight

Witnessing

*He gave me the priestly duty of
proclaiming the gospel of God,
so that the Gentiles might become
an offering acceptable to God,
sanctified by the Holy Spirit.
(Romans 15:16)*

Chapter 29
Use Words – They are Necessary!

ST Francis of Assisi is supposed to have said, 'Preach the gospel at all times; use words if necessary.' Some people understand this to mean that Christians do not need to speak about their faith – they should simply let their good deeds do the talking. Even if St Francis said this (and there is no evidence that he did) he was not denying the value of words. He was a preacher and he trained others to preach – so he must have thought words were important.

What he was doing was exaggerating to make a point. And the point was not that we can preach the gospel with actions *instead* of words but that we need to preach with actions *as well as* words.

Words and actions go together – and unless they agree, our actions, which can speak very loudly, may undermine our words.

Words are needed in order to make sense of our actions – and actions are needed in order to put our words into practice. The word without the act is empty, and the act without the word is dumb.

3-P evangelism

The importance of words and actions working together is highlighted in **3-P evangelism**, a concept that has been used for a number of years but is still relevant.[72] The first **P** stands for '**Presence**'. This means simply living out an authentic Christian life wherever we are, allowing the fruit of the Spirit to grow and be seen in us – 'love, joy, peace, forbearance, kindness, goodness, faithfulness, gentleness and self-control' (Galatians 5:22-23). In this way we bring a Christian presence into any and every situation.

This is important but it is not enough. We also need the other two **P**s, '**Proclamation**' and '**Persuasion**' – and these are done with words.

Proclamation means speaking about our faith. It builds on our godly presence and explains it. Just as Jesus went about doing good and preaching about the Kingdom of God, so we make our presence felt and our proclamation heard. This might be as simple as explaining why we believe what we believe or testifying to what God has done for us.

If proclamation means helping people to understand the gospel, persuasion means helping them to believe it. We should not proclaim the gospel with a 'take it or leave it' attitude. Our aim is for people to respond. Persuasion therefore means encouraging people to seek God – to accept Jesus and to commit their lives to him.

Words are important. We cannot truly communicate the good news of Jesus without them. Paul wrote:

> How, then, can they call on the one they have not believed in? And how can they believe in the one of whom they have not heard? And how can they hear without someone preaching to them? And how can anyone preach unless they are sent? As it is written: 'How beautiful are the feet of those who bring good news!'
> (Romans 10:14-15)

To seek salvation you must believe that Jesus can save you. To believe this you must hear it. To hear it someone must have told you about it. So, use words – they are necessary!

A priestly duty

Gospel words are so important that Paul regarded sharing them as a 'priestly duty'. Peter agreed, saying that as a 'royal priesthood' we are to 'declare' God's praises:

> But you are a chosen people, a royal priesthood, a holy nation, God's special possession, that you may declare the praises of him who called you out of darkness into his wonderful light.
> (1 Peter 2:9)

The Old Testament priests represented God to the people and represented the people to God – they were the go-betweens. As New Testament priests, we are also called to be go-betweens. Not in the sense that we are the only channel through which they can come to him, but by presenting God to people when we live for him and declare the gospel, and by bringing people to God when we help them into a faith commitment. In other words, we do our priestly duty when we practise the **3-Ps** — **P**resence, **P**roclamation and **P**ersuasion.

On the Altar

Paul's particular calling was as a missionary to the Gentiles. This was his priestly duty – and the sacrifice that resulted from it was to be the converts who were 'an offering acceptable to God, sanctified by the Holy Spirit' (Romans 15:16). Paul's words may be a deliberate reference to the prophecy of Isaiah:

> 'They will proclaim my glory among the nations. And they will bring all your people, from all the nations, to my holy mountain in Jerusalem as an offering to the LORD – on horses, in chariots and wagons, and on mules and camels,' says the LORD. 'They will bring them, as the Israelites bring their grain offerings, to the temple of the LORD in ceremonially clean vessels.'
>
> (Isaiah 66:19-20)

But Paul might also be echoing his own words in Romans 12:1, where he called his readers to 'offer your bodies as a living sacrifice, holy and pleasing to God'.

The picture for us is clear. Like Paul, our priestly calling is to proclaim the gospel in our words and actions, and to persuade people to accept Jesus. In doing so we offer them to God, and they offer themselves to him, in total dedication.

What a privilege! What a responsibility!

Chapter 30
Come and See – Go and Tell!

MATTHEW records that at dawn on the Sunday after the crucifixion of Jesus, two women, Mary Magdalene and 'the other Mary', went to the tomb where Jesus had been laid (28:1-10). They were met by an angel who told them that Jesus had risen and invited them to 'come and see the place where he lay'. Then the angel told them to 'go quickly and tell his disciples'.

These women were the first witnesses to the resurrection of Jesus. Their experience sums up what it means to be a witness. It is someone who has experienced something, then tells others about it. It means come and see – go and tell.

Called to be witnesses
Every follower of Jesus is called to be a witness. Some have the gift of evangelism (Ephesians 4:11), but even if we do not have that gift we are not excused from being witnesses. The qualification for being a witness is not a gift but an experience – the experience of knowing Jesus as Saviour and Lord.

If we have that experience we need to be ready to share it. This is precisely what Peter says: 'Always be prepared to give an answer to everyone who asks you to give the reason for the hope that you have' (1 Peter 3:15). We cannot leave this job to the gifted evangelists. It is the privilege of every Christian to know Jesus and it is the responsibility of every Christian to tell others about him.

Learning to be a witness
Every Christian has the basic qualification to be a witness – knowing Jesus. But we also need to learn how better to tell others about that experience. It is a skill that can be learnt, a craft that can be developed.

Every Christian can master some simple steps for sharing their faith. Probably most of us have seen 'before and after' pictures. They illustrate how someone – or something – has been transformed from what they were previously into what they are now. It might be a person before and after plastic surgery, a house before and after refurbishment or a garden before and after landscaping. Witnessing is similar – it is a 'before, how and after' story. It involves saying what life was like before we met Jesus, how we came to know him and what life has been like since. [73]

- *Before I met Jesus*

Even if we do not have a dramatic story of how desperately sinful our life was before we met Jesus, we can usually think of things that were not as they should have been. Perhaps we were selfish, dishonest, lonely or afraid. It is this part of our story that other people can usually relate to, because this may be what they are experiencing.

Of course, we might not have a 'before' story at all. If we grew up in a Christian family or came to faith as a child we may not remember a time before we knew Jesus. Even if this is the case there is still a story to tell. The 'before' may not be part of it, but the 'how and after' can still be told.

- *How I met Jesus*

How we met Jesus can be fascinating to hear. It might have been by going to church as a child, reading the Bible, seeing a film, talking with a Christian friend, experiencing worship, taking part in a course or any number of other ways. When we tell this 'how' part of our story it is important to explain it as clearly as possible and in language that people will understand.

Unfortunately, the longer we have been Christians the more likely we are to speak 'Christianese'! Without realising it we can talk about 'being saved', 'letting Jesus into our heart' or 'being converted'. We may know what we mean, but not everyone else will. They are more likely to understand phrases like 'being forgiven', 'making a fresh start' or 'feeling loved and accepted'.

- *After I met Jesus*

When it comes to the 'after' part of our testimony, we need to talk about the difference Jesus made and continues to make. We might speak about things such as knowing God's forgiveness, experiencing joy and contentment, having a purpose in life, receiving strength, being part of a Christian fellowship and having the hope of Heaven. It is important to show how something in the 'before' part of our story has been changed by meeting Jesus. So, if we are now less fearful and more peaceful, it will be helpful to give an example of when we have felt this way.

Reality and humility
Two important things are needed when telling our story. The first is reality. We need a genuine, up-to-date experience of God, or what we say will not ring true. The following anonymous poem is about advertising but it could easily be about witnessing, illustrating that our words need to be based on reality.

> A lion met a tiger as they drank beside a pool,
> Said the tiger, 'Tell me why you're roaring like a fool.'
> 'That's not foolish,' said the lion with a twinkle in his eyes.
> 'They call me king of all the beasts because I advertise.'
>
> A rabbit heard them talking and ran home like a streak;
> He thought he'd try the lion's plan, but his roar was just a squeak.
> A fox came to investigate – had luncheon in the woods,
> So when you advertise, my friend, be sure you've got the goods!

Now, of course, we do not have to be perfect to be a witness. But we do have to be genuine. We need to communicate a real experience of God, with all its challenges and frustrations, as well as its hopes and joys.

David Watson became a Christian at Cambridge University in the 1950s and was later an influential Anglican vicar and evangelist. He had been brought up in the Church but began to lose interest during his school years. When he left school he spent two years in the military and during that time became an atheist, mainly due to the poor behaviour of the regimental padre. It confirmed his view that there was nothing genuine about Christianity. Then at Cambridge he had a very different encounter. He met a young clergyman at a tea-party. Watson said of him:

> He spoke with simplicity and integrity, and unlike most of the other religious people I had so far met, seemed to speak from a

genuine personal experience. It was not so much what he said, but who he was that got through to me ... My cynicism was disturbed by the apparent reality of his faith. [74]

That was the first step towards David Watson becoming a Christian. A living experience of God is vital when we witness, or we will have nothing real to witness about. Our words will be empty and meaningless.

The second thing we need is humility. Our faith is less about us than it is about God. Izaak Walton was a 17th-century writer whose most famous book is *The Compleat Angler*. It is still read by anglers today. One piece of advice he gave was for them to always face the sun so they would not cast their shadow over the river and scare the fish away. It is all too easy for us to cast our shadow over our story when we witness.

Of course, it is our story so we are bound to feature in it! But we can make the mistake of talking more about ourselves than about God. The emphasis should be on his grace rather than on our goodness, on his work for us rather than on our work for him.

Learning to be a witness can be a challenging process. We can easily make mistakes. But if we persist we will improve. And if we tell our story with reality and humility people are more likely to listen and respond.

Chapter 31
Proclaimers of the Gospel

OFFICERS of The Salvation Army sign a promise called a covenant. It expresses the lifelong commitment they are making, which states:

> Called by God to proclaim the gospel of our Lord and Saviour Jesus Christ as an officer of The Salvation Army, I bind myself to him in this solemn covenant: to love and serve him supremely all my days, to live to win souls and make their salvation the first purpose of my life.

But it is not just Salvation Army officers, or any other full-time Christian ministers, who are called to proclaim the gospel. It is the calling of every Christian.

The good news
To proclaim something means simply to announce it publicly and openly. The word 'gospel' means 'good news'. So proclaiming the gospel means announcing the good news. But what is the good news?

Jesus is described as proclaiming 'the good news of the kingdom of God' (Luke 4:43), 'the good news of the kingdom' (Matthew 4:23) and 'the good news of God' (Mark 1:14). The focus was always on God and his Kingdom. Jesus invited people to submit themselves to the loving reign of God, who, by his grace, would freely forgive them.

After Jesus' death and resurrection the Early Church proclaimed what looks like a slightly different message, 'They never stopped teaching and proclaiming the good news that Jesus is the Messiah' (Acts 5:42).

It was only a difference of words, not of meaning. They were still proclaiming the Kingdom of God, but because it was Jesus who had established the Kingdom and who could make it real in people's lives, the focus was now on him. The two ideas were expressed together when Philip 'proclaimed the good news of the kingdom of God and the name of Jesus Christ' (Acts 8:12) and when Paul 'proclaimed the kingdom of God and taught about the Lord Jesus Christ' (Acts 28:31).

It is often said that John 3:16 describes the gospel 'in a nutshell': 'For God so loved the world that he gave his one and only Son, that whoever believes in him shall not perish but have eternal life.' This verse shows:

- the motive for salvation (God loved us),
- the method of salvation (God gave Jesus),
- the way of receiving salvation (believing in him),
- the purpose of salvation (eternal life).

John Stott gives a helpful summary of the gospel in five simple points:

- What Jesus did: the story of Jesus, especially his death and resurrection.
- Why Jesus came: the prophecies of the Old Testament and the witness of the New Testament.
- Who Jesus is: the only Saviour of humankind and the Lord of all.
- What Jesus offers: forgiveness of sins and the gift of the Holy Spirit.
- What Jesus requires: repentance, faith and public witness. [75]

Witnessing and proclaiming

There is a difference between witnessing and proclaiming. Witnessing is telling what has happened in our lives, while proclaiming is telling what Jesus did in his life, death and resurrection and how this can bring people into a relationship with God. But the difference is not as significant as you might think. They are two aspects of one activity – spreading the good news of Jesus. We see this clearly in Acts 8:25:

> After they had further proclaimed the word of the Lord and testified about Jesus, Peter and John returned to Jerusalem, preaching the gospel in many Samaritan villages.

Peter and John 'proclaimed the word of the Lord', which means they told people the good news of salvation – and they 'testified about Jesus', which means they witnessed to what he had done in their lives. Both these things – proclaiming and witnessing – are aspects of 'preaching the gospel'.

We also see these two aspects of spreading the gospel in the life of Paul. When Paul was arrested and brought before King Agrippa he gave his testimony, and we can clearly see his 'before, how and after' story (Acts 26:1-29). But Paul did more than share his own personal experience. He was a preacher of the gospel. He told people that Jesus had died and had been raised to save them. He also said they should respond by putting their faith in Jesus, receiving the Holy Spirit and living for God.

Defending and confirming

Paul also did something else with the gospel. He told the Philippians he was 'defending and confirming' it (Philippians 1:7). He preached the gospel and shared his testimony but also needed to answer questions and criticisms. This too is part of communicating the Christian message.

When we tell our personal faith story and share the gospel, we should be prepared for the objections people may raise. They might have questions about the reliability of the Bible, about faith and science, about suffering and the love of God, about other religions and so on. If we do not have the answers when people ask us, we should say so. But we should also promise to find out, for many Christian people have thought these matters through, and helpful answers are available.

'Defending' the gospel is like boxing on the back foot, defending against the opponent's punches. But boxers also need to be on the front foot, throwing their own punches. 'Confirming' the gospel is like that. It means giving people good reasons to believe. For example, the fact that there is a creation points to a creator; the existence of love, meaning and goodness suggests there is a source for all these things; and there is evidence for the life and resurrection of Jesus.

These points, and many others, may not prove Christianity beyond all doubt but they do show that our faith is reasonable. Of course, ultimately it is a matter of faith – but these claims do provide good evidence that supports our faith.

Paul's priestly duty was to proclaim the gospel. This is our duty too. We do it by witnessing, proclaiming, defending and confirming the gospel. But, as we will see in the next chapter, how we do all these things can sometimes depend on the people to whom we are speaking and the circumstances in which we find ourselves.

Chapter 32
Opportunity Knocks!

WHEN William Sangster was a Methodist minister in Scarborough in the 1930s, a man in his church took every opportunity to share the gospel. The man was a barber and used cut-throat razors, which were common in those days. On one occasion, with the customer lathered up for a shave, the barber held up the open razor and asked, 'Are you prepared to meet your God?' The terrified man got up and ran! [76]

Some ways are better than others for sharing the gospel. A lot depends on the circumstances.

How do we make good use of opportunities and share the gospel in relevant ways? Paul's experience in Athens gives us a good example. We see it in Acts 17:16-34. He first went to the synagogue to speak to 'both Jews and God-fearing Greeks'. With them he could use Old Testament prophecy and refer to the Messiah when he spoke about Jesus.

Later he encountered some Greek philosophers and had to change his approach. As we look at this approach we see how Paul adapted the message to make it relevant and to make the most of his opportunity.

Common interests

Paul began by responding to their concerns. The people enjoyed 'talking about and listening to the latest ideas' (v 21). Paul was well aware of their religious interests and their fascination with philosophy – so he mentioned the many idols, and in particular the altar to 'an unknown god'. Their quest for knowledge created an ideal opening. In sharing the gospel it is important to be aware of people's concerns and interests. And if we share an interest with them, that is all the better.

Paul linked the Old Testament with Greek philosophy by speaking about God as Creator, Provider and Ruler, and about his relationship to humankind (vv 24-26). Although these concepts were basic to the Old Testament they were also familiar to the Stoic and Epicurean philosophers in his audience. Both groups could agree that God was self-sufficient. The idea that all people shared a common humanity (v 26) and that God's presence was everywhere (vv 27-28) would have appealed to the Stoics in particular. If we can somehow relate the gospel to people's concerns and needs it can help to rouse their interest in our message. So, if someone is interested in sport, we could relate the gospel to sporting concepts such as dedication, fair play and teamwork.

Familiar terminology
Paul also used familiar terminology. In speaking of the 'world' (v 24) and 'life and breath and everything' (v 25), he used terms that were not necessarily found in the Old Testament but which would be familiar to these pagan philosophers. He also referred to well-known Greek writers to illustrate people's relationship to God (v 28). Like Paul, we should avoid using Christian jargon that could confuse people but instead use language and concepts that are familiar.

Although Paul adapted his message to suit his listeners, he was also careful to hold on to his Christian beliefs. For example, when he spoke of humanity being the offspring of God he had in mind the Old Testament concept of humankind made in the image of God rather than the pagan idea that God is everything and everything is God (vv 28-29). The style was adapted to the pagan context, but the substance remained Christian. It is essential that in trying to be relevant we do not lose the truth of the gospel.

Christian beliefs
Finally, Paul introduced specifically Christian ideas. By talking about repentance, judgment, Jesus and the Resurrection, he took his hearers beyond their own beliefs. This was the message they needed to hear, and towards which his comments had been leading. The unknown God could be known in the risen Jesus. However much we try to identify with people and be relevant to their circumstances, at some point we need to introduce them to the heart of the gospel message. Unless we do this, everything else is pointless.

Paul's approach suited the situation. If he had begun by 'preaching the gospel' it would probably have been counterproductive. Instead, he saw the need to prepare the way and to lead his listeners step by step along familiar paths before taking them into new territory. This was the real strength of his approach. Even though it did not work with everyone (verse 32 tells us 'some of them sneered'), others did respond. Some wanted to hear more and a few later believed.

Different approaches

The requirement to make wise use of opportunities and to present the gospel in relevant ways means we may need to take different approaches with different people.

The same applies to different cultures. In some parts of the world it is easier to share the gospel than in others. For example, it is often harder to make the gospel relevant to people in Europe than in Africa or South America. Parts of Europe have been described as post-Christian because only a minority of people accept, or even know, the basic message of Christianity. European society has also been called postmodern, meaning that many people have rejected absolute truth in favour of ideas that seem relevant to them, and have abandoned the idea of any absolute morality in favour of actions that feel right to them. At the same time, though, there is an underlying sense of spirituality, a desire for meaning and a longing for acceptance.

In such post-Christian, postmodern but spiritually sensitive cultures, coming to faith is likely to be a gradual process rather than a sudden experience. One study in the United Kingdom showed that it took an average of four years for someone to become a Christian.[77] During this time they needed to build relationships with Christians, experience the authenticity and relevance of people's faith, and explore the reality of Christianity and the implications of commitment.

Courses such as *Alpha* and *Emmaus*, which allow people to get to know Christians in a relaxed environment and to ask honest questions, have been shown to be helpful in many people's journey to faith.[78]

In whatever context we witness and share the gospel, we will need to be sensitive, honest, understanding and patient. We will also need to realise that it can only be done as we rely on the power of the Holy Spirit, which is the theme of our next chapter.

Chapter 33
And You Will Receive Power

IN 1964 the British Army was involved in a conflict in Borneo. The British troops included some Gurkha soldiers from Nepal who were asked to jump from transport planes into the jungle. They had not been trained as paratroopers, but they agreed to do it as long as the plane flew as slowly as possible and no more than 100 feet above ground level. The British officer replied that planes always flew slowly when dropping troops, but never as low as 100 feet because, if they did that, the parachutes would not open in time. 'Oh, that's all right then,' said the Gurkha sergeant, 'you didn't mention parachutes before!' [79]

For many Christians, witnessing for Jesus is almost as daunting as jumping without a parachute. They feel unprepared and poorly equipped. Certainly witnessing is a challenging task, but Jesus does not expect us to do it without his help. He has given us the presence and power of the Holy Spirit. Just before Jesus ascended to Heaven he told his disciples, 'But you will receive power when the Holy Spirit comes on you; and you will be my witnesses in Jerusalem, and in all Judea and Samaria, and to the ends of the earth' (Acts 1:8).

It was a promise of power to help them achieve his mission. The promise was fulfilled at Pentecost when the disciples were filled with the Spirit. This was vital. And this promise is just as true for us. We will receive power when the Spirit fills our lives and we will be his witnesses.

Jesus and the Spirit
Jesus himself relied on the Spirit's presence and power. The Spirit 'descended on him' (Luke 3:22) at his baptism. He was 'full of the Holy Spirit' as he was 'led by the Spirit into the wilderness' where he was tempted (Luke 4:1-2). He returned to Galilee 'in the power of the Spirit' (Luke 4:14). When he stood up in the synagogue at Nazareth (Luke 4:18-19) he used words from Isaiah chapter 61 to declare that

the Spirit had been given to enable him to accomplish his God-given mission:

> The Spirit of the Lord is on me,
>   because he has anointed me
>   to proclaim good news to the poor.
> He has sent me to proclaim freedom
>   for the prisoners
>   and recovery of sight for the blind,
> to set the oppressed free,
> to proclaim the year of the Lord's favour.
>
> (vv 18-19)

The reality of this statement was seen when 'by the Spirit of God' he drove out demons (Matthew 12:28).

If the Spirit played such a large part in the ministry of Jesus, how could his first disciples expect it to be any different for them? And how can we expect it to be any different for us?

The overflow of the Spirit

The record of the Early Church in Acts shows how vital the Spirit was for its mission. Of course, this mission involved more than just words. The actions and lifestyle of the disciples were part of it too. But it is their spoken witness that we will focus on here.

To begin with, it was the impetus of the Spirit that created mission. On the Day of Pentecost the Spirit-filled disciples were propelled into mission and 3,000 people were saved (Acts 2:1-41). From then on they continued to preach the gospel and the Church continued to grow. John Stott writes:

> We watch enthralled as the missionary Spirit creates a missionary people and thrusts them out on their missionary task. [80]

In the Great Commission Jesus had commanded his disciples to 'go and make disciples of all nations' (Matthew 28:19), but their missionary activity in Acts was more than just obedience to a command, it was an overflow of the Spirit.

When Peter and John were called before Jewish leaders in Jerusalem and told to stop speaking about Jesus, they said, 'We cannot help speaking about what we have seen and heard' (Acts 4:20). As they were filled with the Spirit they just could not stop themselves witnessing!

Do we share the gospel just because it is expected of us, or is it a natural expression of the Spirit's presence within us?

The power of the Spirit
In the Early Church the Spirit not only *inspired* evangelism, the Spirit also *empowered* it. It was the Spirit-energised witness of the first Christians that brought people to faith and made the Church grow.

When Paul wrote to one of the early churches about his work there, he remembered that 'our gospel came to you not simply with words but also with power, with the Holy Spirit and deep conviction' (1 Thessalonians 1:5).

Our words, however wise and relevant, will have little effect on people unless they are spoken in the power of the Spirit. It is the Spirit who shows people the reality of sin (John 16:8), testifies to the truth of Jesus (John 15:26) and creates spiritual life in them (John 3:5-6).

The power of the Spirit not only transforms the people to whom we witness, it transforms those who do the witnessing. Peter, who, in fear, had denied Jesus three times, became a courageous preacher on the Day of Pentecost.

On a number of occasions Acts highlights the bold witness of many of the disciples.

- The Jewish court, the Sanhedrin, 'saw the courage of Peter and John' (4:13) who had been brought before them.
- When they were released, Peter and John met with their fellow believers and prayed that they would speak the word of God 'with great boldness' (4:29).
- In response to this the believers 'were all filled with the Holy Spirit and spoke the word of God boldly' (4:31).
- Following his conversion Saul went to Damascus and 'preached fearlessly in the name of Jesus' (9:27).
- In Ephesus Paul 'entered the synagogue and spoke boldly there for three months' (19:8).

The same is true today. If we find it difficult to speak about our faith, the Spirit can give power to our words and courage to our witness.

The guidance of the Spirit

Early-Church evangelism was also done under the direction of the Spirit. Acts relates some remarkable instances of guidance.

- The Spirit sent Philip to talk to the Ethiopian eunuch, which led to his conversion (8:29-38).
- The Spirit sent Peter to the home of Cornelius, which led to the acceptance of Gentiles into the Church (11:12-18).
- The Spirit directed the church at Antioch to commission Paul and Barnabas, who were then 'sent on their way by the Holy Spirit' on their first missionary journey (13:4).

Modern-day disciples also need to be open and responsive to the guidance of the Spirit. It only happens as we spend time in prayer seeking God's will and committing ourselves to do it.

It is good to know that we are not left to witness by ourselves. We have an important part to play, but the Spirit makes all the difference. He can inspire, empower and guide us. That is why Agape, the global mission organisation, describes witnessing as 'taking the initiative to share the gospel in the power of the Holy Spirit and leaving the results to God'. [81]

This all sounds wonderful – but as we will see in the next chapter, witnessing is not easy. It involves sacrifice.

Chapter 34
A Priestly Duty

THE word 'witness' is a translation of the Greek word *martus*, which is where we get our word 'martyr' from. A martyr is someone who loses their life for the sake of the gospel, but this is not what the Greek word meant originally. It simply meant 'witness', and was used in the sense that we have been using it – someone who has an experience, then tells others about it.

It was not long, though, before some Christians who bore witness to their faith suffered death as a result – and so the word *martus* developed this additional meaning. Stephen was the first Christian martyr (Acts 7:54-60) and there have been countless others since then. Even today, in some parts of the world, Christians suffer death for daring to speak about Jesus. Witnessing becomes for them a sacrificial act.

Of course, this does not happen to most Christians, but there can still be an element of sacrifice in our witnessing. Telling our story can be a costly business.

Sowing the seed
One of the parables Jesus told implies that there is a cost to witnessing and sharing the gospel. It is about a man sowing seed (Matthew 13:18-23). The man uses the broadcast method, which involves scattering handfuls of seed as he walks the field. This enables him to sow the seed quickly over a large area but it also means he cannot be sure that all of it will land on good soil and take root. Sure enough, much of it is wasted as it lands on the path, on rocky ground and among thorns.

In the parable the seed is the message of the Kingdom and the places where it lands represent the kinds of responses people make. Like seed on the hard path, some people simply do not understand the message – it fails to penetrate their minds and hearts, and is soon forgotten. Other people's experience is like seed on rocky ground – they accept the message, but their faith withers away when 'trouble or persecution' comes. The thorny ground stands for people who accept the message but it fails to grow because it is crowded out by 'the worries of this life and the deceitfulness of wealth'.

As witnesses and evangelists we can spend time and energy sharing the gospel with people, telling our story, encouraging them to believe, defending and confirming the gospel, and praying for them – but there is not always the response we would hope for. Even when we witness in the power of the Spirit, we cannot guarantee that people will accept Jesus. God does not force his way into people's lives. In the end the decision is up to them, which means that often people do not respond to the message of the gospel. This can be immensely disheartening.

Perhaps the sense of failure is greater when we see someone respond, then fall away. We might wonder whether we could have been a better witness or whether we should have given them more guidance and pastoral support. This is the sacrificial element of proclaiming the gospel – giving of ourselves but seeing no response, or feeling the pain when someone does respond but does not continue in the faith.

But failure is not the end of the story! The emphasis of the parable is on the good soil. This represents those 'who hear the word and understand it'. The point is that, when we witness in the power of the Spirit, even though not everyone accepts the message and believes, some will. Of course, even this success may not have come easily – it may have involved a great deal of sacrifice. We see this in Edward Henry Bickersteth's song, which imagines Jesus talking to us about our witness for him:

> Come, tell me all that ye have said and done,
>   Your victories and your failures, hopes and fears;
> I know how hardly souls are wooed and won;
>   My choicest laurels are bedewed with tears.
>
> (*SASB* 746 v 3)

Doing your duty

Whether there is failure or success, evangelism can be hard work. Perhaps Paul was thinking of this when he called it his 'priestly duty' (Romans 15:16). Duty is not an attractive word to everyone. It speaks of something that we have to do. It is required because we have been commanded: 'Go into all the world and preach the gospel to all creation'

(Mark 16:15). We have our marching orders! But it is also required because, if the love of Christ is within us, we have an inner sense that we must tell others the good news about him: 'Christ's love compels us, because we are convinced that one died for all' (2 Corinthians 5:14). Evangelism is a duty. It is a responsibility – no matter how hard it might be and whether or not we succeed.

If all this makes evangelism sound like a heavy burden, we should remember that there can be joy in doing our duty. We can witness, not only because we feel we must but because we want to. As we saw in Chapter 33, this is because the Holy Spirit motivates and energises us. But it is also because of what we ourselves have experienced.

The sacrifices of the Old Testament were made as part of the people's covenant relationship with God – they were a response to his grace and mercy. The priestly duty of evangelism is the same. We have experienced the grace and mercy of God and it is our joyful duty to share it with others. We can sense that joy and excitement in the words of Paul as he describes what God has done for us and what, as a response, we need to do for others:

> Therefore, if anyone is in Christ, the new creation has come: the old has gone, the new is here! All this is from God, who reconciled us to himself through Christ and gave us the ministry of reconciliation: that God was reconciling the world to himself in Christ, not counting people's sins against them. And he has committed to us the message of reconciliation.
> (2 Corinthians 5:17-19)

We should also remember what Jesus had said to his disciples when he sent them out on a mission: 'Freely you have received; freely give' (Matthew 10:8). These words are a tremendous encouragement to do our priestly duty – and to do it gladly.

Making disciples

But there is more to our priestly duty. Paul says:

> He [Jesus] gave me the priestly duty of proclaiming the gospel of God, so that the Gentiles might become an offering acceptable to God, sanctified by the Holy Spirit.
> (Romans 15:16)

It is not just about proclaiming the gospel. It is also about helping those who respond to give themselves to God in total obedience – to be a living sacrifice. As witnesses, we not only introduce people to Jesus, we are also to help and encourage them to grow in their relationship with him. The aim of our witnessing is not simply to make converts but to make disciples. This is exactly what Jesus said in his Great Commission:

> Therefore go and make disciples of all nations, baptising them in the name of the Father and of the Son and of the Holy Spirit, and teaching them to obey everything I have commanded you.
> (Matthew 28:19-20)

According to Jesus, making disciples involves bringing people to him and teaching them to obey him.

It has been said that the real fruit of an apple tree is not just apples but another apple tree. The same is true of us as disciples of Jesus and as a living sacrifice. Not only are we to offer our lives to God, but we are to enable others to offer their lives also. He is pleased to accept our living sacrifice and he is pleased when this helps others to become a living sacrifice too.

—— Reflection Eight ——
Witnessing

In the 21st century people in most parts of the world can receive news around the clock. On the Internet, via social media, by phone and through television and radio we can be informed instantly of significant events. Every day we receive many messages as advertisers use all possible means to inform, persuade and convince us to buy their products. Signs and hoardings may challenge us about our political beliefs, invite us to events or inspire us to seek more information online about a particular opportunity.

- *How do you think that living at a time when communication is so readily available should influence the ways we share the good news of Jesus, as individuals and collectively?*
- *What methods have you found best for effective witnessing?*

'We have experienced the grace and mercy of God and it is our joyful duty to share it with others.'

- *Take time to write down your personal story explaining how you first came to know Jesus. You may have shared your story many times but imagine you are speaking to a person who has never met you.*
- *What was your life like before you met Jesus?*
- *How did you first recognise your need of his forgiveness and salvation?*
- *How has your life been transformed since you became a Christian?*

As was suggested earlier in the book, you may not have a dramatic 'before' and 'after' story to tell. Your experience may not fit the stages outlined above. But the important thing is that writing down your story will enable you to study it and examine the way that the witness of others resulted in you finding Christ.

Presence, proclamation and persuasion were considered as a good pattern for witness. It was suggested that we need to be sensitive, honest, understanding and patient in sharing the gospel. Emphasis was placed on witnessing as a natural expression of the Holy Spirit's presence within us.

- *Have these chapters filled you with new enthusiasm to communicate the Christian message? Do you feel better prepared and equipped through the guidance offered?*

The closing chapter of Hebrews contains a lovely prayer that all Christians can make their own.

- *Read Hebrews 13:20-21 and ask God to equip you as you live in obedience to him and glorify his name.*

In Conclusion

THE metaphor of sacrifice, as we saw earlier in this book, is used in the New Testament to shed light on various aspects of the Christian life. It helps us to understand more clearly what it means to offer our lives to God, to pray to him and praise him, to serve him by serving others, to do good, to give and to witness.

Sacrifice lies at the heart of our faith and shapes the way we live. It is vital that we understand this. When Jesus called people to follow him, he made sure they knew what to expect. Life was not always going to be easy. He said they had to 'deny themselves and take up their cross' (Mark 8:34). This is the challenge for us as well.

It means we do not live for ourselves but for God and for others. It means we do not allow self-will to rule us but we make Jesus Lord of our lives. And it means, in Paul's words, that we become 'a living sacrifice, holy and pleasing to God' (Romans 12:1). This is something we should realise right at the beginning of our Christian lives – and something we should keep reminding ourselves of as the years go by.

Faced with this thought, many people might ask, 'Is it worth it?' They may prefer to look for self-fulfilment rather than sacrifice. It is an understandable response. After all, who wants to take the difficult path if there is an easier way? But this attitude fails to appreciate a key principle that underlies the way of sacrifice and self-surrender – that it is the way to freedom and fulfilment.

Jesus made this clear when he called his followers to deny themselves and take up their cross.

He said:

> For whoever wants to save their life will lose it, but whoever loses their life for me and for the gospel will save it.
>
> (Mark 8:35)

He was saying that real fulfilment and happiness come to us along the road of sacrifice. The life 'to the full' (John 10:10) that he came to bring us is found not by seeking it – it is a consequence of self-surrender.

How can sacrifice be the way to fulfilment when these two things seem like opposites? The answer is in Romans 12:1-2. When we become 'a living sacrifice' and are transformed by the renewing of our minds, then we are 'able to test and approve what God's will is – his good, pleasing and perfect will.'

Discovering, and living in, God's perfect will brings genuine fulfilment because that is how we were created to live. God never intended us to live self-centred lives. If we live for ourselves we are neither free nor fulfilled. Instead, we are slaves of our self-will. Our attitudes, actions and aspirations are self-centred, and although they might bring some superficial happiness, ultimately they are unfulfilling.

God made us dependent on him for fullness of life – and the way to find it is to give ourselves completely to him. The secret of life is to place ourselves – all that we are and all that we can be – completely on the altar.

Endnotes

1. Gunton, Colin E. *The Actuality of Atonement* (T&T Clark 1988) p 120
2. Fiddes, Paul S. *Past Event and Present Salvation* (Darton Longman and Todd 1989) p 66
3. Duncan, George B. *Quiet Time* (Ambassador Productions 1990) p 17
4. © Hope Publishing Company, Carol Stream, IL 60188. All rights reserved. Used by permission
5. Booth-Tucker, Frederick *The Life of Catherine Booth* Vol I (IHQ 1893) pp 420-421
6. Bramwell-Booth, Catherine *Catherine Booth* (Hodder and Stoughton 1970) p 16
7. Brother Lawrence *The Practice of the Presence of God* (Spire Books 2004) p 37
8. Carey, George 'A Biblical Perspective' in *Entering the Kingdom: A Fresh Look at Conversion*, ed. Monica Hill (MARC Europe 1986) p 11
9. The *Amplified Bible* tries to make explicit the full meaning of key words in the Greek text, in order to give a better sense of the original author's idea. (A newer edition states we are being progressively transformed – Ed).
10. For example, the *International Standard Version* and the *Complete Jewish Bible*.
11. Sangster, William E. *The Path to Perfection* (Epworth Press 1943) p 123
12. Coggan, Donald *Convictions* (Hodder and Stoughton 1975) p 178
13. Brother Lawrence *The Practice of the Presence of God* (Spire Books 2004) p 36
14. Hybels, Bill *Too Busy Not to Pray* (IVP 2011) pp 64-75
15. Weatherhead, Leslie D. *A Private House of Prayer* (Hodder and Stoughton 1977) pp 7-15
16. Yancey, Philip *Prayer* (Hodder and Stoughton 2006) p 21
17. Foster, Harry (ed) *Through the Year with Watchman Nee* (Kingsway 1977) 2 December

18 Hallesby, Ole *Prayer* (Augsburg Publishing House 1931) p 87
19 *The War Cry* 16 March 1985
20 MacDonald, Gordon *A Resilient Life* (Thomas Nelson 2004) pp 120-122
21 Bosch, Henry G. *Our Daily Bread* (Radio Bible Class 1986) 16 April
22 Luther's *Small Catechism* (Concordia Publishing House 1986) p 20
23 Weatherhead, Leslie D. *A Private House of Prayer* (Hodder and Stoughton 1977) p 12
24 Foster, Richard *Prayer* (Hodder and Stoughton 2000) p 204
25 Quoted in MacDonald, G. *Restoring Your Spiritual Passion* (Highland Books 1986) p 196
26 Ulanov, Ann and Barry *Primary Speech, a Psychology of Prayer* (John Knox Press 1982) p 102
27 Foster, Harry (ed) *Through the Year with Watchman Nee* (Kingsway 1977) 22 January
28 Quoted in Foster, Richard J. *Celebration of Discipline* (Hodder and Stoughton 1980) p 34
29 Quoted in Gibbard, Mark *Twentieth-Century Men of Prayer* (SCM Press 1974) p 41
30 © 1989 Thankyou Music/Adm. by Capitol CMG Publishing excl. UK & Europe, adm. by Integritymusic.com, a division of David C. Cook, songs@integritymusic.com
31 Watson, David *Discipleship* (Hodder and Stoughton 1981) p 133
32 Gunton, Colin E. *The Actuality of Atonement* (T&T Clark 1988) p 201
33 Weatherhead, Leslie D. *A Private House of Prayer* (Hodder and Stoughton 1977) p 8
34 Temple, William *Readings in St John's Gospel* (Macmillan and Co 1950) p 68
35 Gunton, Colin E. *The Actuality of Atonement* (T&T Clark 1988) p 201
36 Hughes, Selwyn *Every Day with Jesus: The Worship of God* (CWR 1978) p 17
37 Quoted in Yancey, Philip *Prayer* (Hodder and Stoughton 2006) p 313
38 Calvin, John *Calvin's Commentaries Vol. 1* (Calvin Translation Society 1847) p xxxvii

39 Many attempts have been made to categorise the psalms. The categories used here were identified by Claus Westermann in *Praise and Lament in the Psalms* (John Knox Press 1981)

40 Foster, Harry *Through the Year with Watchman Nee* (Kingsway 1977) 6 September

41 *The Salvation Army Handbook of Doctrine* (Salvation Books 2010) p 252

42 Foster, Richard J. *Celebration of Discipline* (Hodder and Stoughton 1980) p 112

43 Stott, John R. W. *Baptism and Fullness* (Inter-Varsity Press 1975) p 87

44 Orsborn, Albert *The House of my Pilgrimage* (SP&S Ltd 1958) p 117

45 Quoted in Willard, Dallas *Hearing God* (IVP 2012) p 126

46 Brookfield, Charles Hallam *Random Reminiscences* (1902) (Kessinger Publishing 2008)

47 Howell, Francis *The Characters of Theophrastus* (Josiah Taylor 1824) p 44

48 Booth, Bramwell *Echoes and Memories* (Hodder and Stoughton 1977) pp 13-14

49 Stott, John R. W. *The Contemporary Christian* (IVP 1992) p 345

50 Duncan, Dennis (ed) *J. B. Phillips for This Day* (Word Books 1977) p 116

51 Barclay, William *New Testament Words* (SCM Press 1964) p 21

52 Carlyle, Thomas *Past and Present* (William H. Colyer 1844) p 23

53 Shakespeare, William *The Globe Illustrated Shakespeare: The Complete Works* (1986) p 1,879

54 Houston, James (trs) *The Mind On Fire: A Faith for the Skeptical and Indifferent* (Minneapolis: Bethany House 1997) p 91

55 www.iol.co.za/capetimes/the-man-who-changed-my-life-1533199, accessed 16/09/2018

56 Bramwell-Booth, Catherine *Catherine Booth* (Hodder and Stoughton 1970) p 20

57 Barclay, William *Crucified and Crowned* (SCM 1961) p 19

58 Ibid p 14

59 Quoted in Yancey, Philip *Prayer* (Hodder and Stoughton 2006) p 102

60 Hawthorne, Gerald F. *Philippians* (Word Books 1983) p 120

61 Câmara, Hélder Dom *Hélder Câmara: Essential Writings* (Orbis Books 2009) p 13

62 *The Musician* 16 March 1985

63 Ibid 27 April 1985

64 Quoted in Foster, Richard J. *Money, Sex and Power* (Hodder and Stoughton 1985) p 19

65 Marshall, I. H. *The Gospel of Luke* (Paternoster Press 1978) p 594.

66 Gumbel, Nicky *Challenging Lifestyle* (Kingsway 1996) p138

67 Sider, Ronald *Rich Christians in an Age of Hunger* (Hodder and Stoughton 1978) pp 152-3

68 Ibid p 154

69 Quoted in Vischer, Lukas *Tithing in the Early Church* (Fortress Press 1966) pp 13-14

70 Foster, Richard J. *Money, Sex and Power* (Hodder and Stoughton 1985) p 49

71 Gowans, John *O Lord!* (SP&S 1981) p 29

72 Wagner, C. Peter *Strategies for Church Growth: Tools for Effective Mission and Evangelism* (Wipf and Stock 2010) pp117-123

73 Pattern adapted from Pointer, Roy *Tell what God has Done* (Bible Society 1982) pp10-17

74 Watson, David *You Are My God* (Hodder and Stoughton 1983) p 17

75 Stott, John R. W. *Christian Mission in the Modern World* (Kingsway 1986) pp 41-45

76 Jeremiah, David *Turning points with God: 365 Daily Devotions* (Tyndale 2014) 29 April

77 Finney, John *Finding Faith Today* (Bible Society 1992) pp 24-25

78 Brierley, Peter *Leadership, Vision and Growing Churches* (Christian Research Association 2003) p 18

79 Larson, Craig Brian *Illustrations for Preaching and Teaching* (Grand Rapids: Baker Books 1993) p 36

80 Stott, John R. W. *The Contemporary Christian* (Inter Varsity Press 1992) p 330

81 Greene, Mark *Fruitfulness on the Front line* (Inter-Varsity Press 2014) pp 178-9